Was It Good For You, Too?

Was It Good For You, Too?
30 Years of *Cosmopolitan*

Linda Kelsey

ROBSON BOOKS

First published in Great Britain in 2003 by Robson Books,
64 Brewery Road, London, N7 9NT

A member of **Chrysalis** Books plc

British Library Cataloguing in Publication Data
A catalogue record for this title is available from the British
Library.

ISBN 1 86105 554 4

Edited by Joanne Brooks and Claire Wedderburn-Maxwell.
Designed by Dave Crook.
Photography by Alan Ritchie.
Printed in Spain.

For Susan, proof that the sisterhood is alive and well.

ACKNOWLEDGEMENTS

With all thanks to the women in my working life – the mentors, role-models, colleagues and friends, who never made it seem like work: Deirdre McSharry, Maggie Goodman, Nadia Marks, Marcelle d'Argy Smith, Audrey Stevenson, Marjorie Riley and Emma Dally. Thanks also to Alexandra Pryce and Daniella Scorah for their help with research, and to Joan Tinney for her patience and picture skills.

Contents

FOREWORD

BY EDITOR LORRAINE CANDY

'*Cosmopolitan* is more than a magazine; it is an empire, a brand, a state of mind.' So said *The Times* newspaper in a powerful editorial wishing *Cosmo* a happy 30th birthday in February 2002. That glowing sound bite just about sums up everything you need to know about this Amazon of a publication. Confident, sexy, exciting and glamorous, *Cosmo* is the world's No. 1 magazine, with 46 international editions reaching an awesome 37 million women every month. No other magazine is as famous, as relevant or as influential – it's quite simply the biggest and the best. And this commemorative book is a tribute to that impressive history.

In its lifetime, *Cosmo* has spawned a zillion imitators – none of which has ever matched its power or pizzazz. So, people often ask me, as the current editor-in-chief, what exactly is the secret of *Cosmo*'s enduring success? The answer is simple: *Cosmo* is truly the universal language of love. It's about relationships; and relationships, as any *Cosmo* girl will tell you, are one of the great mysteries of the universe. *Cosmo* is the girl-power guide to getting them right. More insightful and intimate than the best best friend, more of an instant feel-good fix than the bubbliest of champagnes, more saucy and sinful than the most calorific of chocolates, *Cosmo* is the relationship bible for today's modern, young woman. Its fun, fearless and fabulously flirtatious attitude is a manifesto for her life. Launched in the States in 1965 by the legendary magazine diva

Helen Gurley Brown – famously the author of *Sex And The Single Girl* at a time when women were supposed to be staying chaste for Mr Right – *Cosmo* became the voice of a generation. It has empowered several more generations since. This book is as much a celebration of that empowerment as it is of the success of *Cosmopolitan*.

In the UK, *Cosmo* has been groundbreaking and pioneering in its campaigns, it has been taboo-busting in its honest treatment of sex, it has launched careers, pushed back the boundaries with insight into real women's lives, and it's been daring in its portrayal of men (physically and emotionally). Most importantly, *Cosmo* has always been right for its time. I am extremely proud, at the age of 33, to take my place in the magazine's lifetime as the sixth *Cosmo* editor. I can honestly claim *Cosmo* did change my life – with its careers pages encouraging me as an ambitious wannabe journalist at the age of sixteen to chase my dream, despite a hideous lack of qualifications!

I can't imagine a world without *Cosmo* to read in the bath or before bed. Looking through the chapters of this birthday book, I think even our sternest critics (and there have been a few) will be awed by the major (and minor) ways in which *Cosmo* has made an impression on society and touched the lives of its loyal readers. After reading it, I hope something of *Cosmo*'s fun, fearless attitude rubs off on all of you.

INTRODUCTION: COSMOPOLITAN CHANGES LIVES ...

It's just a slick line, isn't it? A slogan. A neat bit of advertising hype. It doesn't actually add up to anything, does it? After all, a glossy magazine is just a bit of fun, something to keep you occupied while you're waiting for your nails to dry (though I never did master the art of turning pages with my teeth). A magazine is what you flick through when you're eating a sandwich at your desk. Or during a bad Bridget Jones moment when the phone refuses to ring – now that's when a copy of *Cosmo*, alongside the ciggies and the Chardonnay, of course, really does come into its own.

But change your life? You cannot be serious. OK, I'm biased. But, yes, *Cosmo* really did change my life – and not just because I spent fourteen years working as a member of the editorial team – starting off as a lowly sub-editor and ending up as *le grand fromage*, the editor (with a few comings and goings on other publications in between) of the No. 1 young women's magazine in the UK.

The No. 1 young women's magazine in the world in fact (not that I can claim any responsibility for that!), with 46 editions worldwide.

To understand how *Cosmo* really did change lives – mine included – you have to look back through the mists of time.

At the beginning of 1972 there was no *Elle*, no *Marie Claire*, no *New Woman*, no *Company*, no *Red*, no *Glamour*, no *In Style*, no *Hello!*, no *OK*, no *Heat*. But *Cosmopolitan* was about to be launched, and that would provide more than enough heat for the time being.

'Girls just wanna have fun' could have been the theme song for the sixties' dolly bird, years before Cyndi Lauper sang her 1983, No. 1 hit. Born in 1952, I'd been too young to take part in the full-on swinging sixties London scene, but not too young to watch and indulge from the sidelines. Like hundreds of thousands of other girls I believed The Beatles in general, and Paul McCartney in particular, were the loves of my life. (The Rolling Stones seemed just too dangerous to even contemplate as boyfriend material, though the older sister of a friend of mine actually slept with a Stone, making her something of a celebrity in my eyes.)

Paul's cherubic face and cheesy grin adorned the walls of my bedroom as I sat on my frilly blue nylon bedspread and dreamed that one day he and I were fated to meet and mate. Then I discovered real boys, and although they never quite matched up to Macca, they were an adequate distraction. My girlfriends and I discussed 'how far' we were prepared to go from one to ten, which took us along a treacherous path from holding hands and kissing (mouth closed was lower down the scale than French kissing) through increasingly risqué activities from 'upstairs outside' to 'downstairs inside' to the unmentionable 'all the way'. The euphemisms we used were coy in the extreme. Experimental we may have been, but our language was far from liberated, an indication that beneath the surface we were deeply unsure of our sexual ground.

Shopping became an equally, if not more absorbing pastime than boys. Saturday afternoons meant one thing – a regular, not-to-be missed pilgrimage to Biba in Kensington Church Street, the coolest clothes shop on the planet, where the stock ran out so fast that every week you could be guaranteed brand new looks hot off designer Barbara Hulanicki's sketch pad. Carnaby Street and Chelsea were simply awesome, and even if you had arrived by bus, you could enjoy the King's Road parade of gorgeous blondes in micro-minis and white patent knee-high boots and envy the ones who got to sit in the back of open-topped sports cars, driven by Terence Stamp lookalikes. It was not unusual to simply jump in if a couple of good-looking guys pulled up and you were lucky enough to be asked if you wanted a ride. It didn't seem at all a risky thing to do.

Saturday nights were disco nights – you prayed you'd pull (pull was the *mot du jour* for a successful pick-up), and if you ended up having had a good snog you'd be in seventh heaven. The sixties may have been permissive for some, but for us adolescents the real revolution was still waiting to happen.

Popstars, boys, shopping and clubbing. Perhaps it doesn't sound much different from the preoccupations of today's teenagers. But for me and most of my schoolfriends the future wasn't in doubt. For us grammar school girls there'd be A Levels, probably, and university, possibly, a job for a bit, then marriage in our early twenties (if it didn't happen by the time we were 25 we'd definitely be on the shelf) and then motherhood and babies. At that point our lives would be, well, sorted, I suppose. Maybe your husband would be the first man you'd sleep with – once you knew engagement was on the cards. Or maybe you'd

even discovered the joys of sex with various partners and without the prospect of an engagement ring dangling before your eyes. What was almost for certain was that you didn't make the first move, you didn't even think of ringing him, you probably didn't pay your way, and he called your dad 'Sir' when he eventually met him. And as far as work was concerned, there was still a residual feeling that career women were likely to end up spinsters. Everyone was having too much fun to bother whether their job was leading anywhere. On the other hand, the boss to whom you were secretary was rather sexy … now that could be leading somewhere.

But there were other stirrings, too. My life, for sure, was about to burst out in all sorts of conflicting directions. I was just seventeen and prematurely on my way to Warwick University. I didn't find the prospect of sex scary but I didn't quite know what to expect of it either. Within days of arriving at university the boy-back-home had been usurped by an aggressively confident love-rat who was something-important-in-student-politics and could explain to me why sit-ins were necessary, why the pigs that ran the place shouldn't be allowed to keep secret files on us, why the bomb had to be banned and how to smoke a joint. He also thought a trip to the student sexual advisory clinic might be a good idea, so I duly got myself down there and, compliant girl that I was, went on the Pill.

> **'This was more like it, this was liberation, this was freedom …'**

This was more like it, this was liberation, this was freedom … Or was it? Looking back I was the antithesis of the sassy, independent girl. Quite simply, having a boyfriend made me feel safe and whole, as had been the case ever since I was twelve years old. (Which is perhaps why an article that cropped up in *Cosmo* years later, entitled 'Why Do I Feel Like Nothing Without A Man?', had such an impact on me.)

And then I went to a student debate and for the first time heard a woman use the word 'fuck' (that's the kind of sheltered upbringing I'd had). The woman was Germaine Greer, she was teaching English at my university, and I was both shocked and extremely impressed. I haven't a clue what was said in that debate, though it was something to do with feminism, a word that was also new to my vocabulary. I was too busy taking in her presence, her power and her passion to actually listen to a word she was saying. And then I read her book, *The Female Eunuch*, and for the very first time started to think about the inequalities between men and women and how life for women might simply not be fair, that the whole thing was skewed in men's favour and something should be done about it. But Germaine's brand of firebrand feminism was too much for me – and at this point I hadn't had any personal experience of what she described, and nor had my consciousness been sufficiently raised for me to notice the 'little woman' traps I constantly fell into.

So I quickly returned to the everyday dramas of life with the boyfriend, quite forgetting that I was supposed to be reading my history books, attending seminars and writing essays. It's a miracle I flunked only one of the three end-of-year exams. Invited to resit the one I'd failed, and having found the boyfriend too hot to handle, I simply dropped out and went home to middle-class comfort with mummy, daddy, my sister and, on my eighteenth birthday, the gift of a brand new mustard Mini.

So there I was in 1970, just eighteen years of age, proud owner of the most coveted status symbol, my own car, already a university drop-out, no longer a virgin, a girl who'd tried the Pill (but come off it because it made me fat and nauseous – in those still early days of the Pill the hormone doses were *enormous*), smoked cannabis (but didn't carry on because that too made me nauseous), living back at home with the same frilly blue nylon bedspread I'd had since I was nine, and asking myself, what on earth next? A job certainly. Journalism, now that sounded exciting. But what could I actually *do* apart from type – a skill I'd learned on a pre-college course so that I could type my essays at university, little knowing that I'd be too busy to bother with that kind of stuff. And then I got an interview for a job as tea girl cum typist on *Good Housekeeping* magazine, with the promise that I could train as a sub-editor if I showed promise. So for two years I worked as assistant to Marjorie Riley and Audrey Stevenson, two kind and competent middle-aged women who treated me like I was a favourite niece and taught me a great deal. They even let me write my first article – a thrilling little piece about service agreements for washing machines – and printed a fictitious poem I'd written about being a useless housewife. Audrey and Marjorie weren't exactly cool, but they were nevertheless my first role models.

At around this time I found myself another boyfriend. But this one wasn't a boy, he was a man. Nine years my senior he seemed sophisticated, smart, funny and confident (all the things I would have liked to be myself, and which *Cosmo* would later show me I could be). He was the life and soul of social situations, enabling me to be my mouse-quiet self. He was also moody and difficult – dominant character traits that didn't manifest themselves until after the honeymoon. We fell in love, he proposed, I said yes. In retrospect I can see that marriage represented the ultimate freedom, the chance to move away from home.

Living 'in sin' was out of the question, my parents would have gone beserk, and anyway he was 28, a lawyer and ready to commit. My mother had also married at nineteen, my sister had married at 21, so for me to marry one month short of my twentieth birthday, one month after the launch of *Cosmopolitan*, and one month before I was to actually move from my job at *Good Housekeeping* to a new position on *Cosmo* (both magazines published by the National Magazine Company) didn't strike me as at all incongruous. I married in bell-shaped sleeves and triple tiers of silk, teamed with a huge wide-brimmed hat; we honeymooned in Rome and Amsterdam and returned to my husband's flat in London's Primrose Hill.

Most of the girls I grew up with married straight from home. But there were plenty of other young women out there forging a brave new world, moving from the provinces to London or from the suburbs to other cities, getting flats together and eking out an independent living. They were the sixties' equivalent of the *Sex and the City* girls. And Helen Gurley Brown, founder of *Cosmopolitan* in the States, was Carrie Bradshaw personified. In 1962 she wrote the international bestseller *Sex and the Single Girl*, making the pretty remarkable statement that having sex and being single were not incompatible, even if you happened to be a woman. It was the success of that book that three years later resulted in the launch of *Cosmo* in the States, and five years down the line a UK edition.

Frankly I was amazed to get the job at *Cosmo*, even though I had bought myself a two-piece green jersey outfit from Jaeger especially for the interview. Editor Joyce Hopkirk grilled me gently and wanted to know how old I was. When I told her I was nearly twenty – in the hope it would make me sound a lot more grown-up than a mere nineteen – she told me not to be so silly. 'You are either nineteen or you are twenty, journalists need to be precise.' That's blown it for sure, I thought. But it hadn't, and I was going to join *Cosmopolitan* as a sub-editor, assisting the chief sub-editor with copy fitting and proof reading, as one of the elite team of eight producing the most-talked about magazine ever.

Even though I hadn't joined the magazine until two months after it hit the news-stands, you'd have had to have been living on Mars to have missed the frenzy surrounding its launch. 350,000 copies of the first edition sold out by lunchtime, partly due to the rumour that there would be a male nude in the first issue. There wasn't. For issue No. 2, which did feature the much vaunted male nude centrefold, the print order had been upped to 450,000 and the magazine sold out within two days. It was a huge, phenomenal, unprecedented success.

So there I was. Newly married woman. Newly inducted *Cosmo* girl. If I'd been born just a few years later – or if *Cosmopolitan* had been around a few years earlier – perhaps I wouldn't have married at such a young age. Perhaps I would have seen that it was possible to live an independent single life, to share a flat and try living without mummy or a man before settling down.

In the opening paragraph of her first editor's letter in the launch issue of *Cosmopolitan*, Joyce Hopkirk said, 'You are that *Cosmopolitan* girl, aren't you? You're very interested in men, naturally, but you think too much of yourself to live your life entirely through him. That means you're going to make the most of yourself – your body, your face, your clothes, your hair, your job and your mind. How can you fail to be more interesting after that?' Well I liked to think that those words applied to me, despite my newly married status, and despite the fact that *Cosmo* had always been targeting readers in their mid- to late-twenties, rather than those like me, barely out of their teens.

'No way, married or not, did I want to be a housewife.'

One thing I already knew for sure (and I have my strict, old-fashioned dad, not just *Cosmo* or feminism, to thank for that), was that work was to be taken seriously. I'd somehow sorted out in my mind that the key to liberation was as much economic as sexual, and that if I wanted some sort of financial independence – rather than relying on my husband for every penny – I'd have to earn my keep. I also knew that a life like my mother's, in which everything revolved around her husband and children, was not for me, however contented she appeared to be. No way, married or not, did I want to be a housewife. And nor did I want to have to ask my husband for money. If all this seems incredibly obvious today, it was still reasonably rare in those days, at least it was in the circles I moved in.

Going from sedate and homely *Good Housekeeping* to brash and buzzy *Cosmo* was mind-blowing. In the early days at *Cosmo* I could have blushed for Britain – a mere mention of orgasms or masturbation was guaranteed to turn my face bright red. As sub-editor I was responsible for checking that words like cunnilingus and fellatio were spelt correctly, which at least gave me the legitimate excuse to look them up and find out what the hell they meant. At home, while my sister and I were growing up, we had never talked openly about sex. When my mother had tried to sit me down for 'a proper talk about grown-up things' her obvious embarrassment made me feel equally squirmy and I flatly refused to allow the discussion on the basis that there was nothing I didn't already know! Although I was now a married woman with a sex life sanctioned by God and society, I still found it impossible to discuss sex openly. What I was discovering was that having a sex life and having good sex are not necessarily the same thing. No wonder *Cosmopolitan* was fast becoming my personal sex therapist.

If my marriage wasn't working, I suppose I could say *Cosmo* was partly to blame. (Years later I'd shrug off the male accusers who'd say things like, 'It's your rag's fault that my wife/girlfriend left me', with the glib retort, 'Are you quite sure it had nothing do with *you*?') But the truth is that what I learned at *Cosmopolitan* did give me the courage to leave my marriage six years down the line. At *Cosmo* I learned that if the man I lived with made me unhappy, I could leave him. At *Cosmo* I learned that if my sex life was lousy, it wasn't doomed to remain that way. At *Cosmo* I learned that I could find a route through feminism that worked for me. I didn't need to become anti-men, but neither did I have to put up with men who didn't regard women as their equals. And neither, most importantly, did I need a man to prove that I was adequate as a human being. At *Cosmo* I found a genuine sisterhood in the women I worked with. At *Cosmo* I found work that was challenging and incredibly good fun. I never got over being shy, but there was a book *Cosmo* published an extract from called *Feel the Fear and Do It Anyway* by Susan Jeffers, which became a bit of a motto. So did *Cosmopolitan* change my life? You bet it did.

That first issue of *Cosmopolitan* aired subjects never previously talked about in a popular women's magazine. Michael Parkinson went on record as saying that 'the most beautiful thing a man can do for a woman …' is to have a vasectomy, and, by the way, he'd had one for his wife Mary. The wonderfully funny Jilly Cooper discussed the famous men she thought would make great lovers, including the unlikely figure of MP Roy Jenkins. Someone confessed to being 'a sleep around girl' and a doctor told readers how to turn a man on when he's having problems in bed.

Joyce Hopkirk, pretty, bubbly, blonde and forthright, and former Women's Editor of the *Sun* newspaper, was the ideal choice for launch editor of *Cosmopolitan*. Joyce was a brilliant networker and knew everyone who was worth knowing, which helped to ensure maximum publicity for the magazine. Anyone she didn't know, but wanted to, she invited to 'the *Cosmo* lunch' which became as hot a ticket as the invite to the *Punch* lunch, a men-only affair, which Joyce mimicked in her own style. At the *Cosmo* lunch powerful, good-looking men were very much the point – from novelists like Frederick Forsyth to David Frost and Michael Aspel. The *Cosmo* lunch was for spreading the *Cosmo* message, with fun and flirting thrown in for good measure.

A newsgirl at heart, a year after *Cosmopolitan*'s launch Joyce decided to return to the world of newspapers. Her successor was Deirdre McSharry, who had worked as fashion editor at the *Sun* at the same time as Joyce and had moved over to *Cosmo* as fashion and beauty editor. Deirdre had red-hair, a fiery Irish temperament (all clichés, but true) and a razor-sharp mind. Her high/low approach to culture meant that Deirdre would embrace all manner of unlikely subjects and present them in an accessible *Cosmo* style. 'Go and reproduce Manet's "Dejeuner sur L'Herbe" in Hyde Park', would be a typical Deirdre command. So off I'd go (somewhere along the way I'd become responsible for the food and homes section of the magazine, as well as the 'bachelor of the month') to find some suitable recipes and organise an outdoor picnic shoot, involving two naked women and a couple of blokes in capes, that mimicked the original painting. The result: a clever, funny, sexy *Cosmo* spread to get people talking, combined with a reference to Manet to get the readers up-to-speed on their art history.

It was Deirdre who introduced *Cosmopolitan*'s famous personal development courses that invited readers to 'Take one Saturday to Change Your Life' and which spun off into dozens of different *Cosmo* careers workshops. It was Deirdre who embraced the fitness craze that was sweeping California and the rest of the States in the late seventies and early eighties, and introduced the idea of fitness, health and well-being to *Cosmopolitan* with its 'Zest' section (for the last eight years *Zest* has been a magazine in its own right). And it was Deirdre who introduced names such as Irma Kurtz, Tom Crabtree, Marcelle d'Argy Smith (later to become editor of *Cosmopolitan* herself), as well as many leading feminist writers.

WHAT THE SWINGING SIXTIES CHICK WAS READING

For a girl who'd grown out of her childhood comics – like Jackie *(my favourite) and* Bunty *(my sister's) – there was barely a magazine to read. She may have graduated to* Honey, *launched in 1961 as a sparky teen monthly for girls who were 'young, gay and get ahead!' (no, NOT lesbian girls, the sixties were never that swinging), which in the mid-sixties featured the Fab Four from Liverpool on the cover with an exclusive interview inside. And* Honey *really was a breakthrough as far as magazines were concerned. It was one of the first to recognise the interests of teenagers, who had finally emerged in fifties post-war Britain as a definable group with ideas and spending power of its own. But although it was youthful, it wasn't radical, it wasn't sexy and by the time you were twenty you'd certainly have grown out of it.*

Perhaps for a faster and more regular fix than Honey *a teenage girl would pick up* Petticoat, Honey's *perky, weekly copycat. Then there was* Vanity Fair, *described by Joan Barrell and Brian Braithwaite in their book* The Business of Women's ▶

Magazines *(out of print)*, as 'a fashion magazine for the shorthand typist' (how patronising does that sound in 2002?). And finally, if the female buyer was a smart twenty- or 30-something desperately seeking a magazine to surprise and challenge her, she might head for* Nova, *a glossy monthly that showcased great writers, truly innovative ideas and radical fashion. But* Nova *was always more highbrow than mass market, and died two years after* Cosmo *was born, in part a victim of* Cosmo's *success.*

Interestingly, the alumni of magazines like Honey, Petticoat *and* Nova *went on to become some of the best-known names in the business. Launch editor of* Honey, *Audrey Slaughter, continued her career by setting up* Over 21 *magazine (now extant).*

Maggie Goodman, the lucky girl who got to conduct that exclusive interview with the Beatles in Honey *became editor of* Petticoat, *deputy editor of* Cosmopolitan *at its launch, invented* Company Magazine *in 1978 and then edited* Hello! *for a period of five years during its heyday.* Honey's *beauty editor, Eve Pollard, reached the pinnacle of success as the First Lady of Fleet Street, editing the* Sunday Mirror *and* ▶

In her twelve years as editor, Deirdre took *Cosmopolitan* to its all-time sales peak of almost 490,000.

By the time I took over as editor in 1985, sales had slipped rather dramatically from that heady high. The management view was that *Cosmopolitan* had become too heavy, too worthy, too feminist and that the time had come to lighten up. I thought *Cosmo*'s current message was pretty on target, but I acknowledged that the magazine was beginning to look more like homework than entertainment. So we redesigned it, improved the quality of the paper it was printed on and introduced more colour pages (today every page in every glossy magazine is a full, four-colour page, but back in the eighties the number of colour pages that we were allocated was strictly limited on a cost per page basis). The changes I made were more a boost of Botox than the full face-lift, but the cosmetic result was evident and had the required effect of increasing sales again.

Becoming editor of *Cosmopolitan*, or of anything else in fact, wasn't something I set out to do. I didn't start with ambition, I just wanted an interesting job. And I don't think that was unusual. As the magazine grew, and the number of staff grew along with it, I kept getting promoted into newly created positions. I was nurtured and mentored all along the way, both by *Cosmo*'s deputy editor Maggie Goodman and by Deirdre McSharry: two smart and generous women who encouraged me to be smart, too. At 25 I was the magazine's features editor and loving every minute of it. And as my marriage was rapidly heading for the rocks, work was a great comfort. In 1978 Maggie decided to launch her own magazine, *Company*. In a way it was like *Cosmo*'s younger sister, and since there was nothing else in the market to rival *Cosmopolitan*, the National Magazine Company thought it might be a good idea to launch a *Cosmo* companion of its own. Maggie invited me to join the magazine as her deputy editor, an offer that was just too good to turn down. During my three years at *Company* my marriage ended and I became a single girl. We sold the marital home, I moved into my own flat, and began to date. Now, finally, at the ripe old age of 26, I really was living the life of the *Cosmo* girl.

After three years at *Company* I went on to help launch another women's magazine called *Options*, before returning to the *Cosmo* fold. The plan at the time was for me to launch and edit Deirdre McSharry's *Zest*, for which she had produced a dummy, but the powers-that-be decided the market was not ready for such a title, and when the vacancy came up for a *Cosmo* deputy editor, I slotted into it.

Looking back at *Cosmo* in the eighties I can see that a *Cosmo* reader of today might see it as earnest and a bit heavy-going. But at the time it was tremendously empowering. Sexual discrimination, sexual harassment and unequal pay were still the norm. I knew how lucky – and unusual – my situation was. Having female bosses who assumed the responsibility for bringing on women younger and less experienced than themselves was an incredible bonus. And I wanted to continue Deirdre's legacy of promoting career confidence in the magazine's readers who might not have the benefit of a Deirdre or Maggie in their own workplaces.

During my five years as editor of *Cosmo* the magazine was faced with the spectre of AIDS, another reason why work, rather than sex, took precedence. Was this the end of sex as we knew it? Was this the end of sex? Eighteen months after my first issue as editor, in which we introduced the subject of AIDS, we came back fighting with our campaign for safe sex and the coverline 'Smart girls carry condoms'.

While 'smart girls' were nipping down to the chemist for a packet of Durex, I was trying to get pregnant by my live-in boyfriend Christian (I must have got better at relationships over the years; at the time of writing we've been together nineteen years). I think my pregnancy was seen as something of a test case for editors at National Magazines, which also published *Good Housekeeping*, *Country Living*, *Company*, *She* and *Harpers & Queen*, all edited by women. Astonishingly I was the first editor in the history of the company to have a baby, and felt obliged to prove it could be done without the magazine falling apart if I took three months off. With Marcelle d'Argy Smith as my deputy editor there was little danger of that. But even in a company in which so many of the top posts were held by women, management was extremely uneasy about senior women, particularly editors and publishers, having babies.

After the birth of my son Thomas, there followed something of a baby boom at National Magazines. It was bound to happen and was simply a reflection of the changes taking place in women's lives across the UK. Women were marrying later and delaying having children. They were beginning to get promoted

then the Sunday Express.

Writers like the novelist Frankie McGowan and multi-faceted media star Janet Street Porter cut their journalistic teeth on Petticoat *and* Honey *and it's where Lynn Franks, perhaps the UK's best-known PR person, started as a secretary. A number of* Nova's *best writers, including Irma Kurtz, who went on to become a legendary agony aunt both in the UK and the US, soon graduated to the pages of* Cosmo.

So in some ways the sixties were a fertile time for magazines and the female talent they nurtured. But Nova, Honey, Vanity Fair *and* Petticoat *apart, mostly what young women could read was a magazine with the word* Woman *in the title.* Woman's Own, Woman and Home, Woman's Weekly, Woman's Realm, Woman's Journal *or the redoubtable* Good Housekeeping, *titles which, like the word woman itself, suggested serious adulthood and serious pursuits such as cleaning and cooking, sewing, mending and knitting, and devoting yourself to your children's mealtimes and your husband's socks. The problem page of* Woman *might just reward you with the odd snippet about sex, but it wasn't much for a girl to go on.* ∎

and were moving into the middle, though rarely the top, ranks of management. Inevitably, by the time they were well established, they would be around 30 years old, exactly the time when the biological clock would start to tick.

Yes, perhaps *Cosmo*'s childcare campaign was stretching things a bit (babies had never been part of the brief), even if many of our readers were exactly the age at which they were starting to think about having children. But right or not, I decided to go with it. And the response from readers suggested that we'd hit the right button.

When I moved on to deal with my new obsession about the work/family balance at *SHE* Magazine, Marcelle took over *Cosmo* and quickly announced 'Sex is Back'. Over the next six years Marcelle made *Cosmo* funnier and more glamorous, kept up the tradition of good writing, introducing new names to the magazine, and even appointed a political editor. Circulation continued to rise – this time dramatically.

In editing this book I have spent a great deal of time poring over the *Cosmo* archives. Marcelle's coverlines were the most outrageous, the most uproarious and the most irresistible. Typical Marcelle: 'Does he understand your body or does he think a vulva is a very safe car?' Of the British editors of *Cosmopolitan* Marcelle was probably the most famous of all, appearing regularly on TV and becoming a pundit on everything from great sex to great reasons for joining the euro.

When Mandi Norwood succeeded Marcelle as editor in the mid-nineties, she introduced a more sensationalist, tabloid-approach that she felt was in keeping with the times, and which she hoped would help to ward off *Marie Claire*. It did. Signature features during Mandi's tenure were 'I survived a serial killer', 'How this little girl from Hampshire became the world's richest porn queen' and 'The Jerusalem syndrome: people who think they're Jesus'. But Mandi also upped the fashion and beauty content, brought back the male centrefolds, and became more sexually explicit. As a circulation strategy, this too succeeded.

As *Cosmo* celebrates its 30th anniversary, Lorraine Candy has been in the editor's seat for two years, overseeing not just the magazine but its successful spin-offs: *Cosmopolitan Bride* and *Cosmopolitan Hair*. *Cosmo Girl*, too, is now an established magazine in its own right.

So after 30 years of amazing success, what is the secret of *Cosmopolitan*'s enduring popularity? It's really not that difficult to suss, though it would be pretty hard to emulate. Despite slight shifts in emphasis to suit the mood of the moment, and even the personal preoccupations and style of successive editors, *Cosmopolitan* has always focused on the things that really matter to young women. What are these things? Love, of course. And sex. And work. And men. And relationships. These are the priorities in young women's lives and in 30 years they haven't changed. What has changed is women's attitudes. Women are more confident in every aspect of their lives. They assume equality rather than having to fight for it every step of the way. They are in no hurry to marry or have kids, though most still want to eventually. They are free to enjoy sex without guilt. But are they still vulnerable? Of course they are. Do they still worry whether he'll ring or notice their cellulite? Of course they do. Do they still find it hard to negotiate relationships? Well that's the nature of relationships. Do they ever have sexual hang-ups? Who doesn't? *Cosmopolitan* continues to stay at the top because it acknowledges these issues are never in or out of fashion, they're simply what matters.

> 'They are free to enjoy sex without guilt. But are they still vulnerable? Of course they are.'

Since *Cosmo* launched in 1972, the landmark changes in women's lives have been tremendous. In the same year that *Cosmo* began, the first refuge for women seeking sanctuary from domestic violence opened in London. We've witnessed the National Childcare Campaign, to improve facilities for the increasing number of working mothers, the formation of The 300 Group, which aimed for equal representation of women in parliament, and rape in marriage being recognised as a crime. From Anita Roddick to Madonna and Margaret Thatcher, we've seen women soar to the heights of achievement. We've had Women's Lib and Girl Power. The Sex Discrimination and Equal Pay Acts. We've explored our sexuality with the help of ground-breaking books like *The Hite Report* and Nancy Friday's *My Secret Garden*, in which women talked openly about their sex lives and their sexual fantasies. We've had The Morning After Pill and Viagra. We've witnessed girls outperforming boys in A Level passes and in 1998, for the first time, gaining more university places, too.

There can't be another glossy magazine that in celebrating its 30th birthday would get its very own leader in *The Times*. But *Cosmo* did under the heading 'Flirty Thirty' – Many happy returns to *Cosmopolitan* Magazine'. And this is what the leader said:

Cosmo is bigger than a magazine, it is a brand, an empire, a state of mind. Brash, engaging, hyperbolic, foolhardy, wilfully witless on occasion in a way that everyone needs. Its greatest compliment has been not only that it has shaped all women's magazines in its image, but that it has transformed a whole genre of men's magazines. The new men and old (enough to know better) lads who disport themselves in *Loaded* and the like owe their attitude to the indefatigable Amazon that is *Cosmopolitan*. She could still teach them a few tricks.

I'm so glad to have been a *Cosmo* girl, both in my work and in my life. And I'm thrilled to be putting together this book, which is not just the celebration of a magazine, but of 30 years of fascinating change in the lives of young women.

Linda Kelsey, Editor, *Cosmopolitan*, 1985-9

THE WORLD ACCORDING TO HELEN GURLEY BROWN

When Helen Gurley Brown launched *Cosmopolitan* in the United States in 1965, she was already famous as the author of *Sex and the Single Girl*, a book that she had published three years earlier, and which, she maintains, was a bestseller because it acknowledged that girls have sex before marriage. By this time married herself – to story editor at 20th Century Fox turned producer, David Brown – it was David who persuaded Helen to turn the philosophy of her book into a magazine, and who suggested *Cosmopolitan* (The Hearst Corporation's ageing and flailing literary magazine) be the vehicle for her ideas. From 1965 to 1997, Helen edited US *Cosmo* on a daily basis and oversaw the international editions of the magazine in between. Since 1997, when she stepped down from the day-to-day running of US *Cosmo*, she has remained working full-time as editor-in-chief of *Cosmo*'s ever-growing roster of international editions – 46 at the last count. On the night that UK *Cosmopolitan* celebrated its 30th anniversary in London, Helen announced to the assembled guests that it was her birthday, too – her 80th. Her energy and her passion are undiminished, and her vision informs every edition of *Cosmopolitan* around the globe. But there is no doubt that the success of *Cosmo* internationally depends

on the ability of individual editors to tune their editions to the sensibilities and interests of their readers in their particular country. UK *Cosmo*, perhaps more than most, went its own way in the early years, adopting a more radical and campaigning stance than its quieter sisters in Europe and elsewhere. In the UK it was also possible to be more sexually explicit than in the US, where in certain states anything too suggestive on the cover would result in it being banned from the supermarket shelves (which is where the majority of US newsstand copies are bought). The day after *Cosmo*'s 30th birthday party I spoke to Helen Gurley Brown about the birth of *Cosmo*.

Linda Kelsey: Can you describe what life was like for you, and for young women in general, at the beginning of the sixties, when you were just about to publish *Sex and the Single Girl*?

Helen Gurley Brown: Up until then, if you were single with no engagement ring in sight, then you might as well go to the Grand Canyon and throw yourself in. If you were single *and* having sex, it was time to stick your head in the oven … Already, after World War II, women were in the workplace big time; that's when feminism really started. The men were at war, the defence plants needed people to work there, and women fitted in. So we can't say there were no career women by the sixties but they hadn't become so prominent or so successful.

There are not very many women who are CEOs or presidents or chairmen of companies even now, but women have terrific jobs. In the early sixties women were doing pretty much what we traditionally did: you could be a teacher, a nurse, work in a store as a sales person, maybe if you climbed the ladder you could be a buyer, or you could be a secretary. But there were no women executives whatsoever.

LK: Most of today's *Cosmo* readers won't have read *Sex and the Single Girl*, or even have seen the movie version starring Natalie Wood. What exactly were you saying about sex and being single that you then went on to put into *Cosmopolitan*?

HGB: I was saying it's not the end of the world if you're a single girl, it's not the end of the world not to have an official mate. It's wonderful to have a man; I think if you're a heterosexual person you want a heterosexual companion, so a woman needs a man, but it doesn't have to be a man that she marries, she just needs a man in her life. And I was saying that women do enjoy sex just as men do, and that had never been thought possible before, you were supposed to close your eyes and think of England, or mentally rearrange the spice rack while you were having sex! So women as equal participants in a physical relationship had not yet happened and those are the two things I was saying. Yes, marriage is OK for some time in your life but it can be later, and sex is enjoyable. I wouldn't push anyone to have sex who wasn't interested, that's nobody else's business – it's like religion, you make up your own mind. But if you are having a sexual relationship it's probably quite wonderful and you don't have to feel ashamed – everybody else is doing the same thing, they're just not out there talking about it. But in my book I *was* talking about it, and I got so much mail: that's how *Cosmo* started. I was trying to answer all the letters, and people hadn't ever had anybody they could talk to before.

LK: The book was an instant success, wasn't it?

HGB: It was, and people always talk about their bestselling books, it's such a cliché word, the 'bestseller', but it was true, and the astonishing thing was that I never got over the thrill of getting a book, any book, published. I felt that was just nirvana! I'd never written anything except advertising copy, so a) to get the contract to do the book, and b) to have it out there, I think that would have been enough for the rest of my life! But it turned out that it was an instant best-seller. The company that I was published with was a new, young company, and they sort of pioneered book promotion. Nobody had ever put authors on the air before, but I was on the big shows in the US, *The Today Show*, *The Tonight Show*, and I was just a real little media sensation, and that helped get the books out of the bookstores. But it was a nice little book, it was very encouraging. It stayed on *The New York Times* list for over six months and it was published in 28 different countries in sixteen languages.

LK: Your book came out a year before Betty Friedan's book, *The Feminine Mystique*, the first book on feminism to capture ordinary women's imaginations.

HGB: They were published close to the same time, and there is no question of Betty Friedan having been the leading voice for feminism at that time. Her message was simply that there is something outside the home that you can do if you want to. It was more than just having a job, however, it was a mindset of men and women; we were supposed to be lesser people, less intelligent. Again she was somebody who hadn't written, she was a scholar. Despite this she got everybody amalgamated. There were focus groups that met all over the country, where women hooked up together and talked about their lives. She and I became friends, she wanted to know if she couldn't get a magazine started and I said perhaps, but why don't you get a book format and see what you can do from there.

LK: So you had a lot in common.

HGB: Her message had nothing to do with the act of sex, it had to do with the act of living, as an equal partner. Women and men were to become more equal in their own minds and in the minds of everybody else. But Betty never wrote about sex, that was not her speciality.

LK: But wasn't *Cosmo*'s message also a feminist one?

HGB: My definition of feminism is that there is equality for both sexes, and not being categorised by your genitals. If you want to be the head of a company and you're a woman, that's fine, and if you want to stay home with the children while *she* works, that's ok. You should do what works for you.

All the time that I was editor, we had a great deal of material on doing well at a job so that you were respected and paid well. It was as much about career as it was anything else. The format was always one major article on sex, one major article on man-woman relationships (*not* having to do with sex but having to do with other things that you were talking about or fighting about), a major article on careers, a major profile of a famous person, and the fashion and beauty pages. It was quite a balanced book. Now I am responsible for 46 international editions and although I can't read Croatian or Japanese or Russian, I can tell from the pages whether they've got the right articles.

LK: Having looked at the magazine over the years, at the changes under the various editors, and thinking about all the other magazines that have been launched against it, it seems that as long as *Cosmo* remembers its basic formula, it does well. If it became obsessed with celebrities it would fail, because it wouldn't do celebrity as well as the celebrity magazines. If it became obsessed with fashion I think the same thing would happen.

HGB: Sure, we all like movie stars, we all like celebrities, but that's not *Cosmo* – a *Cosmo* reader can get that stuff in another magazine. Only from *Cosmo* can she get help with her own life. I was always careful not to use a great deal of fashion in US *Cosmo* because I wanted to use all these other things. There were six big fashion magazines already so we didn't need to be a fashion magazine. To get a lot of fashion just go tell them to put more film in the camera and take more pictures at the particular shoot, but to get an article that's wonderfully written and carefully conceived, that's a lot more difficult. *Marie Claire* is a woman's magazine that talks about the Taliban and geisha women and how funerals are performed in India: that's fine for them, they do it very well. That's not who we are.

LK: Women's lives have changed dramatically over the past 30 years. Where does *Cosmo* fit into this?

HGB: In terms of women changing, I think *Cosmo* would reflect that change but may also have caused part of the change. We've always said that *Cosmo* is a magazine for women who love men and who love children. They are traditional in many ways, but they don't want to get their identity by being somebody's appendage, they don't want to be just somebody's mother, somebody's wife, somebody's lover, somebody's daughter, somebody's sister. We want to achieve something on our own and that has been the credo at *Cosmopolitan* ever since the new *Cosmo* was created 30 years ago.

The big change it seems to me may be that men have now got to put up with us having our other life, so they may not have a wife like they used to have before. I've heard many people say they need a wife because she's the one who does the entertaining, and takes the children to the dentist, and keeps things humming, sends out the Christmas cards. So men don't necessarily have that little helpmate that they did, but in my country anyway they've become better fathers. They spend more time with their children, they do take them to the doctor, they might even attend a parent/teachers meeting and they certainly take their children out to play more than men used to do. They're just so-so at housework, they haven't really got there yet, but if the woman wants to work, and she does, and she brings home a nice pay cheque, it's incumbent upon him to try and help make everything fit together.

CHAPTER 1

WHO SHALL WE PUT ON THE COVER?

The hairdresser, make-up artist and stylist have worked their magic, and the model feels like a million dollars. A glass of champagne and the music have helped her get chilled. She fixes straight ahead with a steady gaze. After a moment she tilts one shoulder forward slightly and delivers a megawatt smile. Next, her eyes narrow just the tiniest fraction and seem to soften. The smile softens too, becomes more knowing, more sultry. Has a deliciously sexy thought popped into her head? The photographer's playing his part – he's been telling her so many times in the last half hour how gorgeous/beautiful/sexy she looks that she's starting to make love to his lens, oblivious to the rest of the team swarming the studio. In fact she barely registers as someone flicks away a stray hair or dabs on more lip gloss. Her expression is sexy, seductive, beguiling, and by the time her image is reproduced hundreds of thousands of times on the cover of *Cosmopolitan*, it's *you*, the potential reader, who's firmly in her sights. *You* are the ultimate conquest and the *Cosmo* cover girl is

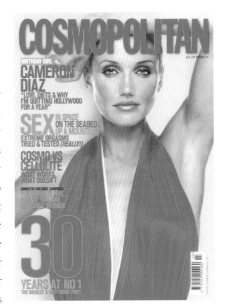

saying to the camera; 'You want me, take me, I'm yours,' delivering her subliminal 'buy me, buy me' message for all its worth.

One thing's for sure. If the model on this cover shoot is thinking shopping lists and what she's going to cook for dinner, or if she can't get the row she had with her boyfriend last night out of her head, it will show when the film is developed. It won't have the magic that's required of a *Cosmo* cover. It won't get past the editor and it will be rejected outright.

In 30 years the message from the *Cosmo* cover girl hasn't changed. It says, 'I'm confident, smart, gorgeous and sexy. I'm flirty and feminine. I'm man-friendly, not a man-eater. And I don't threaten other women. But neither am I pushover. I know what I want – and have a good idea how to get it'. And like the customer in the restaurant who witnesses Meg Ryan's fake-orgasmic performance in *When Harry Met Sally*, the *Cosmo* cover girl makes you want to say, 'I'll have what she's having'. Buy *Cosmo* and perhaps, just perhaps, some of her aura will rub off on you.

Cosmopolitan cover girls don't sneer or snarl and they don't simper. They have to have the best skin, the glossiest hair, teeth that glint, eyes that sparkle. Blondes are probably best. But beautiful brunettes are pretty good, too. A strong jaw is good, little pointy or heart-shaped faces just don't have that power to project. And projecting is what it's all about.

Cosmo has always featured celebrities on its covers, and was doing so long before we became a nation obsessed with the famous. But it has always taken the view that not just any celebrity will do. The celebrity on the cover of *Cosmopolitan* has to resonate with the reader. Paula Yates made the grade in the eighties because she was gutsy, funny and outspoken – as well as gorgeous to look at. Martine McCutcheon achieved cover-girl status in 2001 because not only had she successfully made the transition from soap star to pop singer to much acclaimed Eliza Doolittle in *My Fair Lady*, but because she had agreed to spearhead *Cosmopolitan*'s campaign against domestic violence and talk openly about growing up having to watch her own dad beat her mother on a regular basis.

Many glossy magazines today have given up on models altogether and only feature recognisable stars on their covers – but models still make up the majority of *Cosmo*'s cover girls, and it's interesting to consider why.

The right celebrity at the right time, with the right message for the magazine – and an interesting feature to back it up – will probably shift more magazines than any model. But there are plenty of celebrities who, stunning as they are, do not make great cover girls. Seen in motion, in character and on celluloid, they have the power to mesmerise and move their audience. In still photos those very same stars can look bland, or dull, or piggy-eyed. It could be their mouth that's too big – or their nose that's too small. Or they may simply lack the particular ability to project in still photography.

The more A-list the celebrity, the more control she wants – and she or her publicist may demand everything from the photographer and stylist of their choice to picture approval. A cover which promotes the star in *her* desired image may be at odds with the requirements of the magazine.

Occasionally you come across someone like Cameron Diaz, *Cosmopolitan*'s 30th birthday cover subject. She has the quintessential model girl features (she began her working life as a model), but has moved on to become a huge star with an instant recognition factor. *And* she turned 30 in the same year as *Cosmo*. Perfect!

A magazine cover is like a shop window – if you're not turned on by the display you won't bother to come inside. The correlation between a weak cover image, unispiring coverlines and poor sales is fairly easy to assess. But that also has to be weighed against what your rivals are up to, as banks of competing titles vie for your attention at the news-stand. Millions of pounds and man-hours have been spent trying to turn cover creation into an exact science, but there will never be a fail-safe formula.

In recent years, cover-mounts have become the *bête noir* of publishers, as they spend more and more of their promotional budgets each year trying to out-smart one another with what those in the industry called 'added value', and I call added junk. Put a pair of plastic flip-flops on your magazine and watch sales soar. In fact cover-mounts have raised the cover stakes dramatically. It's hard to judge a magazine by its cover when it's completely obscured by a free T-shirt or a nylon tote bag. With so much choice on offer, readers have become fickle creatures, far more so today than when *Cosmo* launched. Back in the seventies there was both greater reader loyalty and less competition. Your reader may love you truly, madly, deeply, but that free lipstick with *Elle* looks pretty enticing, and the make-up bag with *Marie Claire*, that could be useful, too.

None of this stops an editor angsting over her covers. Because when the flip-flops come out from under their plastic wrap, your cover girl is still staring you straight in the face, and what her look says affects your perception of the magazine, both now and next time you go to buy.

As important as the cover image are the coverlines, the shorthand messages that tell you what to expect between the covers.

When *Cosmo* launched in the States in 1965, Helen Gurley Brown asked her distinguished Hollywood producer husband, David Brown, to write the coverlines for the magazine. In between producing movies like *Jaws*, *The Sting* and latterly *Chocolat*, he continued to do so for the next 32 years. Fortunately for the UK editors he didn't have time to write the British ones, too. It was always one of my favourite jobs, even though it would take what felt like forever to get them right.

Like the cover image, *Cosmo*'s coverlines aim to tease, tempt and tantalise. If they can make you laugh, or at least smile, so much the better. In the early days the editors attempted to balance the sexual with the cerebral, the brawn with the brain, the big-name writers with the Big O. As sexual mores loosened up, coverlines became more sexually explicit. But even way back on its first birthday in 1973, *Cosmo* coverlines were causing controversy. 'I was frigid', ran one line on the cover that was being blown up for a London Underground poster. When the chaps in charge of the Tube realised what it said, they decreed the word 'frigid' had to be covered with a black strip. Unfortunately – but not for *Cosmo* – it was only partly covered, so that the offending word now read 'I was fxxxxd'!'

Cosmopolitan coverlines, from their earliest days, set the standard which other magazines soon adopted – funny, provocative, sometimes outrageous, and written in almost comic-book style. *Cosmo*'s philosophy when it comes to coverlines is more is … more. As a features rather than fashion-led magazine, *Cosmo* has always carried as many coverlines as it can cram in, in the belief that the more the reader has to choose from, the more she'll want to buy

Here is my personal choice of the most award-worthy *Cosmopolitan* coverlines ever:

AWARD FOR COVERAGE OF FOREIGN AFFAIRS

Never close your eyes while making love to Spaniards – the eye-opening reasons (August 1972)

AWARD FOR PO-FACED PONDEROUSNESS

You've got your rights – make what you want of them. We explain the new equality laws and give the very personal views of Anna Raeburn, Helen Mirren, Jacky Gillott and other concerned women (January 1976)

AWARD FOR THE MOST MISLEADING COVERLINE TO MAKE SALES ROCKET

Why Joan Collins needs 12 inches … (August 1984)

AWARD FOR SERVICES TO THE NHS

Smart girls carry condoms (January 1987)

AWARD FOR NO-PUNCHES PULLED

When he says he's a bastard, why don't you listen to him? (November 1989)

AWARD FOR OPTIMISM

We're all at it – SEX is back (October 1990)

AWARD FOR BRIDGING THE GENDER GAP

Does he understand your body or does he think a vulva is a very safe car? (December 1991)

THE 'WE TAKE NO PRISONERS' AWARD

Why men cheat (because they're dick-driven rat people from the Planet Dork – that's why) (January 1993)

THE BOOTS THE CHEMIST COVERLINE AWARD

Shocking New Sex Craze – You won't believe where young women are putting their Alka-Seltzer (January 2002)

From Bond girls to Charlie's Angels, pop stars to R & B divas, supermodels to superstars, *Cosmo* covers have, for 30 years, celebrated the gorgeous, the glamorous and the sexy. What follows is the *Cosmo* cover girls Hall of Fame – and the stories behind the faces.

April 1972

Viv Neves Born in 1948, Neves grew up in Brighton. In 1967 she began working as a waitress in a topless nightclub in London. She became the nude model of the seventies, modelling for *Penthouse*, the *Sun* and appearing nude in an advertisement in *The Times* in 1971. She gave up modelling after the birth of her daughter in the mid-seventies. In 1978 she discovered she has multiple sclerosis, and posed for an advertisement for Action Research into Multiple Sclerosis. She opened the Vivien Neves Modelling Agency in London in the mid-eighties.

December 1972

Ann Turkel Born in 1955 in Manhattan, Ann Turkel took up the stage at an early age. Six feet tall by the time she was sixteen, she was spotted by the editor of American *Vogue*, and shortly after became one of the most sought after models in the US, appearing on the cover of all the top fashion magazines. Two years later, she was discovered in Europe and set out on a successful modelling career there. At age nineteen, Turkel left modelling to work in film, and met her first husband, actor Richard Harris, 25 years her senior. After a fairly long career working in the film and television industry, Ann went to work behind the cameras, and has become a successful photographer. She now spends her time as a spokesperson for animal rights and fundraising for charity.

December 1974

Maud Adams The only Bond girl to star in two 007 films, *The Man With The Golden Gun* (1974), and *Octopussy* (1983), Maud Adams is most famous for these two appearances. In the 1990s she presented a live nightly TV show in her native Sweden and now divides her time between the US and Sweden.

Rene Russo Born in California in 1954, she was discovered at sixteen after attending a *Rolling Stones* concert. Russo has gone from being a successful model to an equally successful actress. She met her husband Dan Gilroy on the set of *Freejack* (1992). Recent films include *Lethal Weapon 4* (1998), and a remake of *The Thomas Crown Affair* (1999) with Pierce Brosnan. She is also in *Showtime* (2002) with Robert De Niro and Eddie Murphy, and *Big Trouble* (2002) with Tim Allen and Stanley Tucci.

May 1976

Margaux Hemingway Born 1955. The granddaughter of Ernest Hemingway, and sister of model/actress Mariel, Margaux's film debut was in *Lipstick* in 1976 (in which Mariel also starred). Despite modelling success and a million-dollar contract from Fabergé, she became an alcoholic, suffered bulimia and epilepsy and had two failed marriages. In July 1996 neighbours informed police that they hadn't seen Margaux (who lived alone) for days, and police broke into her apartment to find that she had died from an overdose of barbiturates.

September 1976

Beverly Johnson As the world's first black supermodel, she now has a beauty empire consisting of eyewear, hair care products and wigs. Her pride and joy is her Bel Air home in California, which sits on a nature reserve.

November 1976

Farrah Fawcett Born in Corpus Christi, Texas, Fawcett was voted the most beautiful woman at High School in the sixties. After a series of roles in TV shows, Fawcett married actor Lee Majors and starred with him in *The Six Million Dollar Man,* posing in a red bathing suit for the publicity poster, which sold more than eight million copies. As a result of the poster publicity Fawcett was asked to star in Goldberg and Spelling's production of *Charlie's Angels.* She divorced Majors and went on to have a

August 1977

seventeen-year relationship with Ryan O'Neal. Farrah Fawcett has continued to make movies and TV shows, and has appeared in the theatre, but she will always be remembered as the original 'Angel' and for the 'Farrah flick' that every girl wanted to copy.

December 1977

Rachel Ward A former model with a dramatic, husky voice, Rachel Ward achieved fame as both a model and actress. She was born in London and perhaps best known for her role as Meggie Cleary in *The Thorn Birds* (1983). She played leading roles in *Sharkey's Machine* (1982), for which she was nominated for the New Star of the Year Golden Globe, *Against All Odds* (1984), and *Wide Sargasso Sea* (1993). She now lives in Australia with actor husband Bryan Brown, and three children, spending her time directing, fund-raising and writing.

February 1978

Raquel Welch Originally a beauty contest winner, Welch broke into acting in 1964, supplementing her wages with modelling. Despite her long list of film credits, she was never as lauded for her acting as for her fabulous body. The movie *One Million Years BC* (1966), promoted with a poster of Raquel as sexy cave-woman in a bikini made of animal hides, is as famous today as it was then. Passionate about yoga, Raquel Welch has gone on to launch successful books and videos and to continue her career as an actress.

August 1978

Barbara Carrera Chiefly celebrated for her sumptuous role as snake fiend Fatima Blush in Bond's *Never Say Never Again* (1983), Carrera achieved fame with her exotic Nicaraguan beauty. Taken on by the Eileen Ford Agency, Barbara was a top model by the age of seventeen, and was one of the highest paid women in the industry at the peak of her career. Carrera was once famous for saying: 'I'll do nude scenes until people give up sex.' She's now single, but has been married three times.

Kim Basinger Another successful model-turned-actress, Basinger was a Bond Girl in *Never Say Never Again* (1983), and starred in *Nine and A Half Weeks (1986)* and *Batman* (1989). After a failed marriage to Ron Britton, she married superstar Alec Baldwin in 1993 (they have since divorced). In the year that daughter Ireland was born (1995), she was voted by *Empire* magazine as one of the sexiest film stars ever. She received a Golden Globe for Best Supporting Actress in 1997 for her performance in *LA Confidential* and more recently starred in *I Dreamed of Africa* (2000), based on the life of Kuki Gallmann. Basinger was chronically shy as a child, and has openly admitted to battling with agoraphobia. She is dedicated to animal rights issues and is a supporter of PETA (People for the Ethical Treatment of Animals).

November 1978

Debbie Harry The blonde known as Blondie, Harry fronted the New Wave band of the same name, pumping out hits such as *Heart of Glass, Denis* and *The Tide Is High* from 1976 to 1982, when the band started to flounder due to her fellow rock musician and lover Chris Stein's ill health. Despite a solo album, Harry stayed off the scene for a while, going on to appear in films and plays, and for a time was a featured vocalist of the *Jazz Passengers*. *Blondie* reformed in 1998 and Debbie Harry still maintains her position as a pop icon.

December 1978

Christie Brinkley One of the all-time modelling superstars, Christie Brinkley was Billy Joel's 'Uptown Girl', and has had four marriages and three children. Born in Malibu, she was always the ultimate 'beach babe', and has endured with one of the longest contracts in the modelling industry - with *Cover Girl* from 1976 to 1996. After a helicopter accident that almost took her life, Brinkley became a businesswoman, selling fitness equipment and anti-ageing skin and hair care products.

November 1980

May 1981

Pamela Stephenson Once a well known comedienne, starring most famously in *Not The Nine O'clock News,* Pamela Stephenson deliberately dropped out of the limelight. She obtained a doctorate in psychology on the psychological effects of fame, and is now known as Dr Pamela Stephenson Connolly. She is married to the great Scottish comic and actor Billy Connolly, with whom she has three children. Stephenson recently wrote her husband's biography, for which she has received great acclaim. She and Billy live in Los Angeles.

September 1981

Jaclyn Smith The only 'Angel' to survive all five years of *Charlie's Angels,* Jaclyn Smith began a long career as a model and actress after having studied ballet and acting as a child. Establishing her film career in relatively small parts, Smith progressed to Broadway productions such as *West Side Story*. She also appeared in major commercials for products from *Max Factor* to *Martini*. After three failed marriages, she now lives with her two children, and has written the beauty book *The American Look*.

May 1983

Isabella Rossellini Daughter of *Casablanca* star Ingrid Bergman, Isabella Rossellini is famed for her natural beauty, which gives her looks far younger than her age. Rossellini was born a twin in Rome, in 1952. She became spokesperson and primary model for Lancôme for fourteen years. She has acted in films such as David Lynch's *Blue Velvet* in 1986 and *Fearless* in 1993. Rossellini was once married to film director Martin Scorsese, and has dated both Gary Oldman and Mikhail Baryshnikov. She now lives with Jon Wiedemann and her two adopted children, Roberto and Elettra. After being fired by Lancôme for being considered too old to promote their cosmetics, she launched her own cosmetics and skincare line, Manifesto.

Annie Lennox Trained as a classical musician, Annie Lennox studied the flute at the Royal Academy of Music. With musical partner, guitarist Dave Stewart, Annie Lennox formed the Eurythmics in the early eighties and went on to have one of the most successful musical careers in British rock history, with non-stop hits such as 'Sweet Dreams' and 'Here Comes The Rain Again'. Continually manipulating an unpredictable image, the Eurythmics were always at pop's cutting edge. Lennox has also succeeded solo with albums like *Diva*. After her collaboration with soul divas Aretha Franklin and Stevie Wonder, Lennox had two children with husband Uri Fruchtman. She is a vocal activist for Shelter, Greenpeace and AIDS charities.

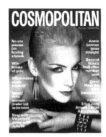

October 1984

Elle MacPherson Born in Sydney in 1964, Elle became an eighties supermodel. Elle is known as 'The Body' for her fabulously athletic figure and six foot frame and still models today. She is also a successful businesswoman – her lingerie was recently launched in the UK – and has a son with her Swiss financier partner Arpad Busson. She was formerly married to the fashion photographer Gilles Bensimon.

January 1985

Bob Geldof An Irish journalist turned singer/songwriter, Geldof sprang to fame with The Boomtown Rats, who produced hits such as 'I Don't Like Mondays'. Spurred to action by watching news reports of Africans dying of hunger in Ethiopia, Geldof persuaded nearly every big name in rock music to join with him in forming Band Aid and selling the single 'Do They Know It's Christmas', to raise money for the cause. The Live Aid event raised millions. His wife Paula Yates left him for rock star Michael Hutchence. Since the death of Paula, Geldof has raised Yates' daughter by Hutchence, as well as his own three daughters. He has recently released a new album entitled *Sex, Age and Death* and lives with French actress Jeanne Marine. He was photographed for the Christmas cover of *Cosmopolitan*, with his daughter Fifi Trixiebelle, in the guise of 'Santa Bob'.

December 1986

October 1987

Cindy Crawford Cindy was born in 1966 in Illinois and studied chemical engineering on an academic scholarship, but left, aged nineteen, to pursue her modelling career. She became one of the first major supermodels and has been on the cover of more than 600 magazines worldwide. Her trademark mole is a mark of beauty, though for her first appearance in *Vogue* it was deliberately airbrushed out. She owns a piece of Planet Hollywood and her own production company, Crawdaddy Inc. She has appeared in music videos for George Michael and Jon Bon Jovi and was formerly married to actor Richard Gere. During their marriage, the couple took out a newspaper advertisement proclaiming their hetero-sexuality, after the media suggested that their marriage was a sham. Now an active gay rights supporter, Cindy is also settled with Rande Gerber and has had two children with him.

January 1989

Claudia Schiffer Born in 1970 in Rheinberg, Germany, Schiffer was introduced to the US by Guess? advertisements and is one of the world's best-known supermodels. She has been on more than 400 magazine covers throughout the world, and was part-owner of Fashion Café restaurants with Naomi Campbell, Christy Turlington and Elle MacPherson. She is also a spokeswoman for breast cancer and a volunteer for UNICEF. She was engaged to magician David Copperfield but the relationship ended and in 1999 she became engaged to Green Shields Stamp heir and playboy Tim Jeffries. When that relationship also ended, she married producer Matthew Vaughn.

July 1990

Madonna Born Madonna Louise Veronica Ciccone in 1958 in Michigan, USA; she is one of the most successful female singer-songwriters of all time: by 2001, her albums had sold 153 million copies worldwide. Often controversial, three of her videos were banned by MTV: 'Justify My Love' (1990), 'Erotica' (1992) and 'What It Feels Like For A Girl' (2001). She has also starred in a number of films, most notably *Desperately Seeking Susan* (1985) and *Evita* (1996). Her 1998 album *Ray of*

Light won three Grammys. She also won a Golden Globe for Best Actress in a Motion Picture (Musical or Comedy) for *Evita* in 1996. Madonna was married to the actor Sean Penn between 1985 and 1989. In 1996 she gave birth to daughter Lourdes Maria Ciccone Leon, fathered by her personal trainer Carlos Leon. In August 2000 she had her second child, Rocco, and in December 2000 she married his father, the director/writer/producer Guy Ritchie, at Skibo Castle in Scotland.

Izabella Scorupco Born in 1970 in Poland. As a girl Izabella moved to Sweden with her mother. She studied drama and music, and at the age of seventeen was discovered by a Swedish film director who cast her in the movie *No One Can Love Like Us*, which made her a local teenage idol. She went on to become a successful model in Sweden and throughout Europe. In 1989 she launched her pop career with the single, *Substitute,* which went gold along with the subsequent album, *IZA*. She returned to acting in 1994, with the lead role in the Swedish film *Petri Tears*. She starred with Pierce Brosnan in *GoldenEye* (1995) and her latest films are *Vertical Limit* (2000) and *Reign of Fire* (2002).

December 1995

Karen Mulder Born in 1968 in the Netherlands. Karen launched her career at the age of seventeen, after coming second at Elite's 'Look of the Year' contest, 1985. She has modelled for Victoria's Secret, Calvin Klein, Ralph Lauren, and Chanel. She was once tipped to marry Prince Albert and is now retired from modelling.

August 1996

Liz Hurley Born in 1965, she went to ballet boarding school aged twelve, and won a scholarship to the London Studio Centre. She first came to fame when she upstaged boyfriend Hugh Grant at the premiere of *Four Weddings And A Funeral*, wearing a side-split Versace dress barely held together by designer safety pins. She has appeared in a number of films,

March 1997

including *Austin Powers: International Man Of Mystery* (1997), and *Bedazzled* (1999). From 1986 to 2000 she was in a relationship with Hugh Grant; they set up Simian Films in 1994, in partnership with Castle Rock Entertainment. In 1995 she was chosen as the model for Estee Lauder. She produced her first film, *Extreme Measures*, (starring Grant) in 1996. She recently had her first child, naming producer Steve Bing as the father, though so far he has refused to accept responsibility.

January 1998

Teri Hatcher Born in California in 1964. Teri Hatcher studied acting at the American Conservatory Theatre in San Francisco, while taking a degree course in mathematics and engineering. Best known for her role as Lois Lane in the TV series *Superman,* she has also starred in the Bond movie *Tomorrow Never Dies* (1997) and *Spy Kids* (2001). She has been married to actor Jon Tenney since 1994 and they have one daughter.

October 1998

Natalie Imbruglia Born in 1975 in Sydney to an Italian father and Australian mother. At the age of two she began dancing, and got her first job as a TV extra in a Japanese commercial. At seventeen she was offered a two-week trial to play Beth Brennan in the Australian soap *Neighbours*, and stayed for two more years. After leaving the show she moved to London to pursue a singing career, and had the mega-successful hit 'Torn', from her album *Left of the Middle*. She has dated racing-car driver Jacques Villeneuve, singer Lenny Kravitz and actor David Schwimmer.

October 1999

Geri Halliwell Born in Watford in 1972 of Spanish/Swedish parents. Geri Halliwell rose to fame as Ginger Spice, one of the pop phenomenon that was The Spice Girls. She left the group in 1998 and launched a solo music career, releasing three singles ('Mi Chico Latino', 'Lift Me Up', and 'Bag It Up') that went to No. 1 in the UK. She has written an autobiography, and become a UN Goodwill ambassador. These days she is blonde, not ginger, and has lost her curves through yoga.

Britney Spears Born in 1981 in Louisiana. As a child Britney attended dance classes and won gymnastics competitions. She went to New York's Off-Broadway Dance Centre and the Professional Performing Arts School, and after a series of television commercials and stage appearances, joined the Disney Channel's *The Mickey Mouse Club* at the age of eleven. She was a member for two years and then signed to Jive Records in the late nineties. In 1999 she released her debut single, '... Baby One More Time', which sold 13 million copies. She is the first solo artist ever to have a No. 1 album and single on the Billboard Charts at the same time with a debut. She starred in the film *Crossroads* (2002) with Dan Aykroyd and Kim Cattrall. Having famously stated that she wants to remain a virgin until she is married, everyone thought she'd marry long-term boyfriend Justin Timberlake from NSYNC. Her relationship with Justin is now over.

January 2000

Cameron Diaz Born in California in 1972, the daughter of a Cuban-American father and an Anglo-German mother. Diaz started modelling at the age of 16. After five years travelling the world to pursue her modelling career, she returned to the US and was cast opposite Jim Carey in *The Mask* (1994). Her films include *A Life Less Ordinary* (1997), *My Best Friend's Wedding* (1997), *There's Something About Mary* (1998), *Being John Malkovich* (1999), *Charlie's Angels* (2000) and *Shrek* (2001). In 1995 she was chosen by Empire magazine as No. 13 in the '100 Sexiest Stars in film history'. She was with the video producer Carlos de la Torre for five years, actor Matt Dillon for two years, and is currently dating actor Jared Leto.

March 2002

CHAPTER 2

YES! YES! YES! YEEEES!

Sexual intercourse began in nineteen sixty-three
(which was rather late for me) –
Between the end of the *Chatterley* ban
And the Beatles' first LP

'Annus Mirabilis', Philip Larkin

The beginning of the sexual revolution, which Philip Larkin ironically (or perhaps wistfully) described in his poem, 'Annus Mirabilis', neatly sums up the rush towards a new expression of sexuality that began in the sixties. But for women it was the contraceptive pill, launched in 1961, that made the first real difference. Freed, for the first time, from the fear of unwanted pregnancy, young women made their first tentative steps towards sexual liberation.

Not that getting hold of the Pill was a simple matter. When it was first introduced the Pill was only officially available to married women. It wasn't until 1967 that Family Planning Association clinics were allowed to give contraceptive advice to the unmarried as well (although with an engagement ring and application for a marriage license as proof, they might have got away with being prescribed the Pill a fortnight in advance of the big day!). Free contraception was not introduced until 1974.

By the time the sixties were getting into full swing, it was already the seventies. *Cosmo* signalled both sexual revolution and sexual revelation. Young women had never before had a forum in which sexual issues could be openly discussed. There was this wonderful feeling that Everything You'd Ever Wanted To Know About Sex But Had Been Afraid To Ask was about to be addressed. And it wasn't just the mechanics, but the whole business of how women felt about sex in the context of their relationships with men, that could finally be brought out into the open. Orgasms bagged the headlines, but *Cosmo* was never merely a how-to manual. The magazine recognised that you couldn't even begin to talk about sex to women without talking about relationships.

Sex, we acknowledged right from the start, can be joyful, disappointing, funny, serious, elevating, depressing, loving, lustful, passionate, sensual, noisy, quiet, dangerous, angry, tender, rough, gentle, deliciously slow or fabulously fast. And even with the same person it might be all of these things — at different times. Good technique can enhance good sex, but the sum of any sexual encounter would also depend on how you felt about the person you were with, and how he felt about you.

Cosmopolitan didn't encourage promiscuity — it was never remotely ambivalent on that particular subject. Of course you have the right to say 'yes', we told the readers … and how dare anyone label you a slag for exercising that right. But alongside that right to say 'yes', also came the right to say 'no', we insisted, to refuse to be coerced into sex, to turn down a man you don't fancy, or trust, or simply want to get to know a bit better. Sexual liberation, according to *Cosmo*'s philosophy, was about freedom from traditional sexual stereotyping. About the right to claim — as well as to give — pleasure. About questioning the whole premise on which notions of 'good' and 'bad' girls were based. And about embracing sex, love and passion with enthusiasm and with gusto, free from guilt.

Were we obsessed with orgasms? Well we certainly paid a lot of attention to them, but that's because of all women's sexual hang-ups, orgasms were the biggest hang-up of all. And if it wasn't the only sexual issue, it was certainly the one that dominated the early years of the magazine.

Freud, who famously — and despairingly — asked, 'What *do* women want?' had a lot to answer for. He came up with the notion that clitoral orgasms were 'immature', and that a woman should strive for 'mature' vaginal orgasms. This was a notion that stuck well into the sixties. The fact that most women were not achieving orgasm during intercourse – and that most men didn't have a clue what to do about it – led to a lot of unhappiness. Many of these women felt there was something wrong with them, but they were ashamed to discuss it with their partners – and terrified of the consequences. And since many would fake orgasms – to please their partners or hide their 'frigidity' or even to 'prevent their husbands leaving them' – the men were often left completely in the dark about their partner's frustration. And so the cycle of dissatisfaction would continue.

By the mid-sixties women were enjoying far greater sexual freedom. In experiencing and experimenting with more than one sexual partner before marriage, they were learning a lot more about their bodies, and depending on their levels of sexual confidence – and how good their lovers were in bed – enjoying greater sexual satisfaction. But still, for many, everything in the bedroom was not rosy. Then in 1966 William Masters and Virginia Johnson (he was a gynaecologist and she was a psychology researcher), published their groundbreaking work *Human Sexual Response*. Their research freed women from the myth of the vaginal orgasm – and proved that all orgasms during intercourse are triggered by stimulation of the clitoris, even though the resulting feelings may stimulate rhythmic contractions deep inside the vagina. Great news for women, maybe, and repeated often in the early years of *Cosmopolitan*, but not until Shere Hite came along in 1977 with her famous *The Hite Report* did we really get to the truth about women and orgasm.

Over 3000 women answered her comprehensive questionnaire about both the pleasures and frustrations of their sexual experience. *Cosmopolitan* couldn't wait to print the results. Although the overwhelming majority (88 per cent) claimed to be orgasmic (i.e. they could achieve orgasm given the appropriate sexual stimulation), only some 30 per cent of the orgasmic women climaxed during sexual intercourse. Moreover, the majority of the 70 per cent of women who did not have orgasm during intercourse felt guilty about it!

And that sums up why for some, at least, the words *Cosmopolitan* and orgasm became synonymous. There was a lot to understand, a lot to learn. Not only could the magazine help readers deal with their sexual insecurities, it could reach men as well. Not surprisingly, *Cosmopolitan* has always had the highest male readership of any women's magazine. Down the years men, too, could learn about what makes women tick both in – and out of – bed, and I can't count the number of times men have told me, 'Everything I ever knew about women, I learned from *Cosmopolitan*'.

But if *Cosmo* ever got carried away with a subject, you could always trust Irma Kurtz to put things back into perspective. In 1980 she wrote:

> Most letters on the topic [of orgasm] are like those from the thirty-three-year-old woman who wrote to say that she had never had an orgasm; her first marriage had foundered on the issue, or so she thought, and she was afraid her current relationship would go the same way. To her, and others in her position, it is important to know that it is not at all difficult to have orgasms. In fact, in our society it is becoming rather hard to avoid them, or at least to avoid filmmakers' orgasms, novelists' orgasms and even journalists' orgasms. If you haven't found the button to push, there are illustrated books in most libraries …
>
> So any couple, any person, keen to have orgasms, can avail themselves of a wealth of instruction … If however, as so often is the case, the woman is keen to learn, but the man thinks he knows it all, then her first step towards orgasm will be to persuade him of his ignorance. Or she will learn to masturbate – that is, induce orgasm in herself by herself – to show how it is done, if she wants to show him …
>
> Inability to achieve orgasm during intercourse or simultaneously with the partner, is, for many women who write agony letters, one of the silliest and most artificial hang-ups since we stopped wearing girdles. If there is a couple who unfailingly have mutual orgasms during intercourse, I do not envy them for they must have their lovemaking down to the breathtaking excitement of a motorway rest stop. Nor do I melt with pity for women who do not have orgasms during intercourse. So what? If you have orgasms before intercourse, or after it, if you enjoy making love, if you like your lover a lot, I do not see it matters a damn …

Orgasms summarily dismissed … but only, of course, for a month or two.

So how has *Cosmo*'s sexual coverage evolved in the three decades since its launch? In the seventies, *Cosmopolitan* approached sex with serious-minded sincerity. When it came to sexual specifics, the magazine deferred to the experts, rather than trust the topic to a mere journalist or to personal testimony. The article I have chosen to reproduce here illustrates the point. The subject is oral sex, the expert is one Dr Wardell Pomeroy (co-author of *The Kinsey Reports*), and the Q & A format is formal, professional, clearly designed to inform and certainly not designed to titillate. There are no illustrations … and no hint of humour. This textbook approach would look wholly out-of-keeping in today's *Cosmopolitan*, but despite the 30-year time lag, I think the information contained in it would, for the most part, be as educational today as it was then. The difference is this: in 1975 a no-holds-barred article on oral sex still had the power to shock. Today no one would bat an eyelid.

In the early eighties there was a sense that we could move on from sexual facts and look more obliquely at sex and relationships. Marcelle d'Argy Smith started to write for the magazine, musing regularly about sex and men and being single. Unlike the sexperts who told you what to do, Marcelle just described what she saw and what she felt and distilled her personal experiences, with warmth, humour, and sometimes – when describing men – anger or exasperation. But in a small piece entitled 'This could be the end of something small', she perfectly encapsulated 'the morning after the night before'. Funnily enough, she didn't even mention the word sex …

In the mid-eighties, just at the time when I became editor, we were suddenly hit by the issue of AIDS. Charmingly carefree pieces like 'This could be the end of something small …' suddenly felt worryingly irresponsible. Not only had concerns about the health implications of the Pill begun to surface, suggesting the increased likelihood of a range of problems from thrombosis to breast cancer, but the Pill offered absolutely no protection at all from the possibility of AIDS. Of course women weren't about to stop having sex, or embarking on new relationships, but there was a very strong feeling that relationships might somehow have to be redefined. We heard stories about AIDS, in certain parts of Africa, affecting men and women equally, and we were fearful that it might happen here too. But what could we do? The biggest contribution we felt we could make was to campaign for safe sex, and in January 1987 greeted in the new year with the coverline 'Smart girls carry condoms'. Written by Denise Winn, the article pulled no punches. Sex went and sat quietly on the back burner for a couple of years, waiting for the moment when it could re-surface – with a vengeance.

Of course AIDS remained a problem, but it never became the epidemic of dire prediction in the West. Marcelle d'Argy Smith, newly appointed as editor, after my departure to relaunch *SHE*, boldly announced 'Sex Is Back' in October 1990. Everyone knew that it had never actually gone away, but Marcelle's declared intention was to bring it flamboyantly out of the closet in which it had been hiding. What *Cosmo* discovered in the early nineties was its sexual sense of humour, with coverlines that made you laugh out loud and articles that would have you giggling all the way to bed. Cartoonist Gray Jolliffe's illustrations to a feature entitled 'The care and feeding of his erection', were clever and outrageous. Kate Saunders' description of sex as 'more slapstick than high drama' for the feature 'Get ready for great sex' (March 1991) was an indication of *Cosmo* sex to come.

During the second half of the nineties, under the editorship of Mandi Norwood, and continuing under the influence of Lorraine Candy, *Cosmo*'s sex coverage has grown both in size and explicitness. In the seventies *The Hite Report* described how although most women masturbated, many felt ashamed or guilty, and had never talked about it to anyone. In February 1999, under the heading '35 ways to send a naked man insane with desire', readers were encouraged to 'Pull up a chair, open your legs, and challenge him to a mas-turbating competition. First one to come buys the winner a gift from Tiffany. (Make sure you cheat!)'

Sexual humour is still very much part of *Cosmo*'s 'Passion Package', the name given to the section where you can pick up the latest sex tips and techniques. '*Cosmo*'s top 10 Outdoor Sex Positions' (June 2001), for example, featured The Balcony Balance in which readers are instructed to 'take in the view in this bent-over-the-balcony bonk.' On a raunch-rating out of five, with a tester who tried it out in Florence, it rated full marks ... and the comment 'If only Romeo and Juliet had known about this one ...'

The 'car-ma sutra' position exhorts you to 'Rev up your ecstasy engines, because this motorised missionary position gives new

What makes the humiliation worthwhile is when she licks it off!

meaning to the term man(hood).' Raunch rating: 4/5 – 'It'll drive you crazy'.

So what exactly is going on here? For those brave enough to try – and why shouldn't *Cosmo*'s fun, fearless readers be up for it – the sex tips are, well, useful. The humour has an almost old-fashioned 'nudge, nudge' quality to it, and rather reminds me of all those *Carry On* films in which everyone spent the entire time making lewdly suggestive remarks, accompanied by winking and digging elbows into people's ribs. And somehow it deflects, and softens, the explicitness of the copy. Sex has become an A-Z of alliteration – through carnal cuddles to naughty nookie, quivering quickies and taboo trysts. It's certainly a far cry from the language of 1972, in which Jill Schary, introducing *Cosmo*'s first ever article on orgasms, declared, 'The ability and right of women as well as men to enjoy sexual expression and satisfaction is as important and relevant a subject today as any other physical ability or civil right'. How might that be put it in 2002? How about 'X-rated ecstasy, out-of-this world orgasms and pulsating passion guaranteed. Why? Because you're worth it'.

Cosmo's 21st-century take on sex is clearly G-spot on for its current readership. But alongside *Cosmo*'s instructional – and often funny – sex tips, are the (increasingly popular) reader confessions. Women behaving badly seems to be the theme. To be able to brag 'I slept with my best-friend's husband on their wedding day' or 'I gave my boss a blow-job on the way to a meeting,' is a peculiar distortion of the concept of sexual liberation. It's lad's mag smut with a sex change. And I thought we girls were better than that.

GREAT MOMENTS IN SEX

1977 – *Cosmo* reports on *The Hite Report*'s main findings

- Women are orgasmic, but necessarily through intercourse
- Women who are non-orgasmic during intercourse often feel guilty about it
- Women feel more inhibited than men about discussing masturbation
- Women still find it embarrassing and difficult to make their sexual needs known to their lover

1982 – *Cosmo* reports on the Grafenberg (G) Spot

Dr John Perry, a psychologist, and Beverly Whipple, a nurse working in the USA, discovered a trigger spot inside the vagina, which, when firmly pressed, may cause ejaculation in some women, as part of the process of orgasm. Named for the gynaecologist who originally wrote about this controversial phenomenon in 1950, Perry and Whipple speculated that the area corresponded to that of the prostate in the male. They also suggested that perhaps as many as 25 per cent of women experiencing difficulty in climaxing may be hindered because they feel that if they have an orgasm, they will urinate. Laboratory analysis of the ejaculation produced by the Grafenberg reflex showed that it was definitely not urine and was similar in content to semen (but without the sperm!)

1992 – *Cosmo* reports on CAT (coital-alignment technique)

Devised by Manhattan psychotherapist Edward W Eichel, the CAT – a variation of the missionary position – was said to not only increase the chance of coital orgasm for women but also tends to 'bring on that rarest of ecstasies, simultaneous orgasm'.

His study of 43 of the men and women who tested the method was published in the *Journal of Sex and Marital Therapy*, and concluded that before being taught Eichel's technique, only 23 per cent of the female subjects said they reached orgasm during intercourse. But afterwards the figure jumped to 77 per cent. After printing Eichel's step-by-step guide to CAT, *Cosmo* readers reported equally positive results.

1998 – *Cosmo* reports on 'The Ultimate Sex Secret' – his G spot

The male 'G' spot is a dimple the size of a five pence piece right at the base of his penis, where the penis and scrotum emerge from his body. 'The area,' said the article, 'is mission control for a series of sensitive nerve endings that radiate throughout the pelvis and buttocks, and when gently pressed right at the point of orgasm, it will send your man into another universe of pure pleasure'.

Don't blame me. They're your hang ups!

Oral sex

Dr Wardell Pomeroy, distinguished researcher in the field of human sexual behaviour and co-author of *The Kinsey Reports*, has written several major studies of human sexuality. Dr Pomeroy believes, as we do, that it is important to deal openly with all aspects of our sexual lives. Only knowledge, he feels, can reduce unhappiness and guilt, and give us the freedom to express ourselves fully.
August 1975

Oral sex is as old as the history of humanity. It is depicted in an Egyptian papyrus of 1700 BC, while the art and literature of ancient Greece and Rome, and of India, are replete with depictions of it. Biologists tell us that it is part of our phylogenetic heritage, meaning that it occurs commonly in lower mammals and even in birds and reptiles. Comparative studies of human behaviour show that oral sex is practised by most societies. Only in the West, shaped by the Judeo–Christian tradition, has a code evolved that denies discussion of this technique.

Oral sex is one of many patterns of sexual behaviour which have become socially taboo in spite of its prevalence at all levels of society. Many couples are concerned about the propriety of having oral sex. As a psychologist specialising in marriage guidance and sexual problems, I know that the restraints that so often accompany oral sex can cause difficulties for people of all ages, married and unmarried. My concern in treating them is not whether they do or don't have oral sex, but rather to help them feel that they have the freedom to express themselves in this way if they want to without guilt or fear. Freedom is the key word because my experience tells me that lack of freedom keeps people from enjoying sex and prevents them from overcoming their problems, whatever they are.

In the hope that people will be helped to achieve more freedom if they understand more about the subject, and helped to express their love more completely, I have tried to summarise in the questions and answers that follow what we know about oral sex.

Q What is oral sex?

A It seems self-evident, but some people are surprisingly ignorant of the separate acts that comprise it, and the vocabulary that goes with them. When a male places his mouth on a female's genitals, that is cunnilingus. When the female's mouth is placed on the male's penis, that is fellatio. These two acts can occur simultaneously.

Q How prevalent is oral sex?

A In 1953, Dr Kinsey's studies indicated that about 50 per cent of married males and females performed oral sex. The acts occurred much less often, as might be expected, among older married people born before 1900, and were much more frequent among younger couples. Today there is no doubt that oral sex occurs in at least 80 per cent of the better educated population, and somewhat less among those at a lower level of education. The difference is not a matter of what is learned in school but simply the prevalence of taboos against oral sex at lower social levels.

Q Do most couples make oral love simultaneously or separately?

A Both. It is widely believed that simultaneous oral sex is a usual practice, but there are physical reasons for preferring separate positions. The difficulty of simultaneous oral love-making is an almost inevitable inability to concentrate, which can be distracting and sometimes even disruptive. One partner becomes so interested in his, or her, approaching orgasm that he/she forgets the other or else concentrates on the partner at his/her own expense. Another difficulty is that the mouths of both partners may not be in the best positions for maximum sensory pleasure.

Q If simultaneous oral sex is not the best way to engage in this kind of love-making, what is?

A There are many variations, of course, but if it is to be cunnilingus, the best position is for the male to lie between the female's outstretched legs, facing her, with his head at the level of her genitals. If the act is to be fellatio, the best position is for the female to lie between the male's legs, as he did in cunnilingus, but somewhat higher up so that the penis will be pulled upwards rather than downwards.

Q What happens if one or both partners feel oral sex is distasteful because of taste or odour involved in the act?

A When one partner is aroused sexually, all sensory thresholds go up, so that normal taste and smell reactions are diminished. Consequently, if there is an initial distaste, it may well disappear if both partners are already aroused when oral sex is initiated. The one most aroused is likely to do the initiating. The distaste, it may be added, is a psychological reaction. If ordinary bodily hygiene is practised by the partners, there is nothing physically repulsive about either the taste or smell of genital secretion.

Q Should oral sex be only a prelude to intercourse, or should it be practised as an end in itself?

A Many people commonly use it as a petting technique before intercourse. Others, however, usually (or always, in some cases) achieve orgasm through oral sex. For women who are multi-orgasmic, oral sex can lead to further orgasms. Since males are not usually multi-orgasmic, orgasm through fellatio usually stops sexual activity, for a time at least.

Q How about swallowing the semen in fellatio? Does the male expect and want the female to do it?

A Most males prefer the female to swallow it, and may interpret a refusal to do so, however wrong it may be, as a reflection either on them or the act itself.

Q Is there any harm in swallowing semen?

A None whatever. Its chemical constitution is similar to saliva in the mouth.

Q Many people seem to think there is something unclean about human genitals. Is there?

A No more than any other part of the body would be, as long as normal habits of cleanliness are followed.

Q Can venereal disease be transmitted through oral sex?

A Yes, it is possible, but only under special circumstances. There must be a lesion or sore in or around the mouth in order for germs to penetrate the mucous membrane. Gonorrhoea is considerably more difficult to contract orally than is syphilis. There is probably no difference between fellatio and cunnilingus as far as the possibility of contracting VD is concerned.

Q If one partner thinks oral sex is 'dirty' or wrong or just generally distasteful and the other wants it, should the reluctant partner make an effort to overcome the unfavourable attitude?

A I find people who make the effort to change their attitudes succeed in feeling only neutral at first. Positive feelings come later. But, again, the key word is freedom. If an individual *feels free* to have oral intercourse, and then finds it unpleasant, at least there has been an exercise of options and no compulsion or pressure.

Q Is there a double standard in oral sex?

A In common discussion of the subject, it's true that we often hear about a woman's ability to perform fellatio skilfully, but rarely do we hear men extolled for the same virtue. Unfortunately, in spite of the liberation movement, we still live in a male-dominated society, where male attitudes establish the mores. Men are much freer in talking about being fellated than about performing cunnilingus, because, in their world, this is part of the male machismo. Many women have told me what poor lovers their men were in oral sex, but said they hesitated to educate them for fear of hurting their egos. We can only hope that women will become more forthright in telling or showing men what they really enjoy.

Q How often, by comparison, is oral sex performed in relation to other kinds of intercourse?

A There are no solid data available to answer this question. We know only that variation is tremendous. Oral sex may be a once-in-a-lifetime act for some people, or it can be an occasional part of love-making. At the opposite extreme are those who have sex in no other way. It is safe to say that, commonly, oral sex is a prelude rather than an end in itself. The point is that whether or not it ends in orgasm is unimportant.

Q What are the pros and cons of oral intercourse?

A I believe that oral sex is a significant, extremely intimate act of the most loving and giving kind. In many respects it is more intimate than 'ordinary' intercourse and provides the rewards that such deep intimacy can give. On the other hand, it is paradoxically a rather lonely activity because the partners are not face to face.

Q What do men and women most often ask about oral sex when they're talking to doctors?

A They seem to be mostly concerned about whether the act is 'normal', or a 'perversion'. I tell them it is perfectly 'normal'. A few people, less so now than in the past, appear to connect oral sex somehow with homosexuality and fear they may be exhibiting homosexual tendencies if they enjoy or want oral sex. Occasionally, I find patients who are fearful that they may get so accustomed to oral sex that they will not want anything else. That rarely occurs, however, and even if it did, it would hardly matter unless one part-ner in a relationship was so accustomed and the other wasn't.

Q Do women tend to feel more guilty about oral sex than men?

A That may have been true in the past, although there is no proof of it, but certainly part of today's sexual enlightenment is not only the increase in oral sexual activity, but a consequent decrease in guilt feelings about it. Recent books, readily available to the public, have done a great deal to erase or dimin-ish guilt about oral sex, as well as the other varieties of sexual behaviour.

Q When the female is performing fellatio, can she subtly hint that she would like cunnilingus?

A As in any other act, the partner who desires a certain activity has the responsibility of communicating that desire to the other person. The trouble, as my patients constantly tell me, is that people often have a great deal of difficulty communicating. I suggest that it ought to be done in a positive, not a negative way. If a woman says, for example, 'Oh that feels good – and I like it even better here,' she will get far better results than if she says, 'Stop, you're hurting me,' or 'You're clumsy'.

Q What do you do about your teeth during oral intercourse?

A This is far from being as irrelevant as it may sound. There are some males who have a fear – often concealed or even unknown to them until their first experience with fellatio – of being bitten. However, most men do not like 'raking' by the woman's teeth. It's a more gentle touching that they want. Lips can be used as a cushion for the teeth.

Q Should the scrotum and/or the testicles be manipulated during fellatio?

A Some men are very sensitive about their testicles and prefer to have neither scrotum or testicles touched. You'll just have to experiment gently to find out whether your partner is one of those. If he isn't, such manipulating, if gently and lovingly done, can add greatly to a man's enjoyment of the act.

Q I have heard of the word 'irrumation'. What does it mean?

A It is a word sometimes used to distinguish fellatio, in which the female takes the active role, from the kind of movements where the man makes pelvic thrusts and so takes an active role. That is irrumation.

Q Fellatio doesn't do a thing for me, and from my female standpoint, I find it a tedious bore. Do some women really like it, or do they just do it to please men?

A Yes, a great many women thoroughly enjoy it. There are those who argue that fellatio is a man's pleasure as cunnilingus is a woman's, but I think both sexes can enjoy each activity.

Q How long does it take a woman to achieve orgasm through cunnilingus?
A That's difficult to answer because of the great variation in women's orgasmic responses. Some women never have orgasm at all by this means, while others are so excited by the act that they are in orgasm almost from the moment oral intercourse begins.

Q Would a man prefer oral sex to ordinary intercourse?
A No, because oral sex does not fulfil all of a man's needs. Both the man and the woman have a responsibility to teach the other partner what kind of sex each one likes best and how to perform it for the greatest satisfaction. What is best for one is not best for all.

Q Do men want to lie back passively and enjoy fellatio?
A Some women have suggested that men do, indeed, enjoy lying back and assuming what seems to them a superior position while the woman plays what appears to be an essentially subservient role. While that may be true in some cases, no generalisations can be drawn about such chauvinistic attitudes. There is as much variation among men as among women. Some men enjoy the passive role at all times, others only on occasion, while still others always play the active role (irrumation) in oral sex.

Q Does it take men longer to reach orgasm than women in oral sex?
A That's another question that's hard to answer because sex is so much more than the physical act. How long it takes a man to reach orgasm depends on his psychological reactions to the act, just as it does with women.

Q Can oral sex be helpful in dealing with an impotent man?
A The great problem a man faces when he is impotent is the fear of failure. He attempts to will an erection, and he develops a tendency to become a spectator at his own performance, constantly worrying about his failure to have an erection and worrying about what his partner may be thinking. To overcome these feelings, the partner needs to eliminate any pressure she may be exerting over him through insisting that he have an erection.

Q Why do I feel guilty after oral sex, but never after intercourse?
A You are responding to age-old taboos. My opinion is that what is done between consenting adults in private should never result in guilt.

Q What part does fantasy play in oral sex?
A First, let me make an observation about fantasy itself. In my practice I have seen how often fantasy becomes a problem. For some reason, many of my patients seem to think that fantasising about another person during intercourse of any kind is evidence of unfaithfulness and may result in eventually acting out the fantasy. Unmarried people seem to worry as much about this one as the married ones. To the contrary, I find that the ability to fantasise, no matter what it is, can be helpful in enjoying any sexual activity. But oral sex allows somewhat more freedom to fantasise because there is no intrusion of the reality of face-to-face contact.

After such a conducted tour through oral sex, filled with physical acts and facts, I may have left some readers with the impression that this is what sex, or at least oral sex, is all about. On the contrary, I think women and men should always remember that the largest and most important sex organ we have is our brain. Psychological factors are more important in sex than physical ones.

The ability to love another person, to communicate with him, to be abandoned with him, to be free with him, to feel the sheer exultation of erotic feelings – that is what sex is all about. I hope the answers I've given to these questions will help people relax and develop their sexual potential. It's worth the effort. ■

'This could be the end of something small.'

Waking thoughts on one of those mornings
after the night before …
Marcelle d'Argy Smith
March 1984

What am I doing here? How much wine did I drink? Do I have any codeine? Did last night really happen? Isn't the back of his neck vulnerable? Aren't his shoulders nice and masculine? What do I mean nice? Is he sleeping as deeply as it sounds? Did we say anything embarrassing to each other? Is he moving? Will he wake up? Shouldn't I creep to the bathroom? What do I look like? Why wasn't I more prepared? Doesn't my mouth taste awful? Can I slide out of this bed without waking him? Will he open an eye and see me? Why aren't I more confident of my body? Will I wobble as I walk? Why was I so anti-exercise? Why didn't I go on a diet? Does it really matter at this point? Why didn't I sleep on the side near my clothes? What are my suede trousers doing on the window-sill? Why don't I go to the bathroom now? Did he stir? Which door is it? Why wasn't that door marked 'Cupboard'? Who designed this room? Do I flush the lavatory and wake him up unromantically or do I act like a charming slut? Does he like sluts? Whose toothbrushes are these? What is that bottle of Channel 19 doing there? Does he still see her? Is she good in bed? Is she good out of bed? What am I thinking about? Why isn't the hot water working? Where's the Nivea? How do you regulate these damned taps? What do you put on a scald? Shall I wash everywhere? Did I imagine he'd have a bidet? Isn't baby powder a nice touch of innocence? What's he doing with it? Don't I look rather good, considering? Don't my eyes have a certain shine? Shall I use his razor? Aren't my legs a little rough? Will he be mad if I use his razor? Will he notice if I've used it? Isn't a relief that I had my hair washed yesterday? Does he like tits? Can I get back into bed without him noticing? Shall I douse myself with Chloé or is that too terribly obvious? How high is this room? Why does he keep that photograph of his ex-wife and baby on the walnut chest? Is she a natural red-head? Isn't that baby about 12-years-old now? Does my stomach look flatter when I'm lying on my back? What'll we do when he wakes up? Will I get to like him? Does he have plans for any part of this weekend? Will this ruin a friendship? Do I need a lover? Can I cope with one? Will he rush out of bed to play tennis at nine o'clock? Will he drive me home, leave the engine running and say 'I'll be in touch'? Why don't I go now and leave a note saying 'This could be the end of something small'?

Does he always sleep this soundly? Is he really turning over and smiling with his eyes closed? Will the men delivering my new sofa be livid I'm not in my flat? Isn't it good to have this arm thrown gently over me? Isn't it wonderful it's starting to rain? What else can he find to do in this weather? Do I care about Chanel 19? Or where my boots are? Or if I'm slightly overweight? Shall I wake him?   Or is he going to sleep till lunchtime because *he* can't face the morning after?   ■

Smart girls carry condoms

The condom may not be ideal contraception but in the battle against AIDS and other sexually transmitted diseases, it's the best protection we have.
Denise Winn
January 1987

'There is no such thing as safe sex,' said Dr Connie Wofsy, co-director of an AIDS project for women in San Francisco, at a recent conference. The message had to be blunt. For it is only slowly starting to sink in for women that casual sex is now a very risky business.

In parts of Africa where AIDS is rife, equal numbers of women and men are affected. And a now much-quoted recent study of military recruits in New York found that eight in 1,000 men and six women in 1,000 between the ages of nineteen and 25 are carrying the HIV virus (Human Immuno-deficiency). A recent report from America shows that it is increasing there at a greater rate in heterosexuals than homosexuals. By the end of last year, a small number of women had already died from the disease in this country.

Estimates of the number of carriers in Britain vary wildly from the Department of Health's 30,000 to more than 300,000. It is more likely to be somewhere near 100,000. Most are still gay men and intravenous drug users, but experts are convinced that it will spread through the general population soon, as a sexually transmitted disease, unless we take steps to stop it. Many gay men are bisexual and drug users do have sex, too.

Further complications

Carriers have a 10 to 30 per cent risk of developing the killer disease within the first five years but ultimately 70 per cent or more may succumb. Even if they don't get the actual disease, many will suffer neurological problems and face premature senile dementia.

Women carriers have to be advised not to become pregnant, as not only is there a 50 per cent risk of giving AIDS to the baby but also a greatly increased chance of developing it themselves while their immune systems are depressed during pregnancy.

The facts are alarming. Yet, despite the panic (The Terrence Higgins Trust, a charity which informs and advises on Aids, receives nearly 60 per cent of its calls from worried women), there hasn't yet been a great deal of positive action. Perhaps the main reason is that for women who are not in monogamous relationships, the single most protective measure against AIDS, apart from celibacy, is the cruelly condemned condom. 'According to the most recent information, condom use is going down,' says Kaye Wellings, research officer at the Family Planning Association.

Condoms are not exactly conducive to the carefree sexual activity which, post-Pill, we seem to assume is our right. Yet in the current climate, the condom has its definite pluses for any who engage in casual sex or who aren't sure of their partners' sexual activities elsewhere. It also protects against other sexually transmitted diseases that hit women hardest, like genital warts, which are linked with an increased incidence of very aggressive cervical cancer.

The diaphragm is by no means in the same league and the Pill and the IUD are not in it at all. None of these can protect against AIDS. 'Friction during sex causes minute abrasions so if you cover those with semen, there is considerable danger,' says Dr William Harris, consultant in genito-urinary medicine at St Mary's Hospital in London. The AIDS virus is passed through blood, semen and vaginal secretions, with anal sex an extremely high risk.

So why have we still made no measurable move to welcome back the condom? According to several experts, it seems that it is men rather than women who are really resistant to reinstating the rubber. Janet Green, organiser of the women's campaign against AIDS for the Terrence Higgins Trust, says, 'Many women say that their boyfriends won't use condoms, so they fear they will be rejected if they suggest it'.

Sheaths are safer

This picture is reflected at genito-urinary clinics in London where high numbers of people attend for HIV testing or advice. Dr Tom McManus, consultant in genito-urinary medicine at Kings College Hospital says, 'Our biggest problem is that heterosexual men won't use the sheath and so women don't bother asking them. We can have a sensible mature discussion about safer sex with women and with gay men, but heterosexual men laugh at us. They still say things like contraception is the woman's responsibility or that the condom reduces sensitivity. They have got out of the habit of expecting to use one.'

Dr William Harris of St Mary's puts it very directly, 'I believe the use of condoms is to a large extent, in the control of the female. At present, it isn't socially acceptable to suggest a condom. But women only have to start to insist and it will become acceptable'.

To be effective, both as a contraceptive and as a protection against disease, the condom must be rolled on only when the penis is erect, not before. Any air must be pressed out in the process and then it must be pulled down fully. After sex, the man must withdraw quickly and hold on to the condom to prevent any leakage. Fine condoms are as protective against disease as thicker ones. However, a new condom that is self-sealing at the base should be available at the beginning of the year. Spermicides, particularly those with five per cent or more of Nonoxynol-9 as the active ingredient, are a sensible optional extra. Not only do they zap undesirable alien organisms as well as sperm but they add lubrication which stops the condom tearing. (Vaginal lubricant is an alternative when the woman is dry but never use anything oil-based, as that rots the rubber.)

Condoms are 85–98 per cent safe as contraceptives when used correctly but they can also be used as additional protection when necessary. As for the complaints about loss of sensitivity, it is interestingly the non-users who most protest and not those who are accustomed to using them. Spontaneous, condoms are not – but we can't have everything, or so it seems.

More important even than that, perhaps, as an explanation for our resistance, is the feelings about sex that condoms bring out into the open. The woman who starts carrying condoms in her bag is having to admit to herself that she may be in the market for casual sex. Whereas the encounter that occurs when she is unprepared can be passed off as unprecedented passion. A woman who is in a steady relationship, but one where monogamy is only given lip-service or less, may feel that suggesting a condom is tantamount to admitting or accusing one or other partner of having sex with someone else.

'These are difficult issues but in the end they need to be confronted,' says Dr Helen Ward of St Mary's who, with social anthropologist Sophie Day, is studying the success of health education for women. It is, perhaps, all part of taking a deeper look at what our sexual relationships are really about. For even condoms cannot offer 100 per cent protection against disease. So-called 'safe sex' means no penetration at all, but touching, stroking and mutual masturbation – not the currently accepted content of sexual encounters.

Redefining relationships

Someone who has already had to reassess what sexual relationships are about for himself is Jonathan Grimshaw, one of the founders of Body Positive, which started as a support group for gay men who were carrying the AIDS virus:

I was one of the first ones to have the test and I was devastated,' he says. 'This was at a time when even gays thought AIDS was a rare risk, much as heterosexuals do now. We thought it was only those who had loads of sex and used lots of drugs who could get it. It was very easy and tempting to distance yourself from the threat in this way, because it was not a nice message that AIDS is around and that you might have to change your lifestyle.

It took me a long time to adjust to not having penetrative sex any more. But I thought about what I used sex for. It isn't just about gratification, it's about self esteem, making relationships, social life and, in fact, those things don't actually require sex. I realised that why I thought penetrative sex was the be-all and end-all had a lot to do with what I thought was expected of me. There is this macho thing in the gay world, too.

I began to see safe sex not as a limitation but as an opportunity to be close in other ways and to put more emphasis on communication, kissing, touching, talking. I am not saying it is always easy. But I do feel

I am showing respect for my own life and other people's. There are considerable rewards in that.

Many women are also now rethinking what sex means to them. 'I am very aware of AIDS and everything else now,' says Shelagh, a 26-year-old teacher. 'I really have to be attracted to someone very strongly as a person before I will consider having sex with them. I have realised it can be so empty otherwise and it just isn't worth the risk. When I want closeness, it isn't from casual sex that I'd ever get it. If there is no one important in my life, who I can get to know first, I'd rather have cuddles with a friend.'

'I think we need to look at what we as women want from sex,' affirms Sophie Day. 'Penetration can often be good for the man rather than the woman because it is not necessarily about real closeness. The scare of sexually transmitted diseases can be a real ally in getting sexual activity right for the woman, too. We don't have to take risks with our bodies to suit someone else. It is up to us to act on that.' ■

Get ready
for great sex

Silly noises, crazy positions, unusual odours … forget
what it says in romantic novels – real-life sex is
all about piggy grunts and loud squelches.
Kate Saunders
March 1991

Tenderly, he caressed her silken thighs. Then,
quivering with barely suppressed passion, he thrust his proud manhood into her
orchid-like portals … with a long, loud squelch. Yes, that's right. A squelch. You
may have been led to believe that the sexual act was something
fragrant and refined, but the reality is infinitely less dignified. Sex rumples your
hair, smudges your make-up, acquaints you with another person's body fluids
and invariably makes your bedroom smell like the lair of about 60 horny,
unwashed badgers.

The fact that sex is messy and often more like slapstick than high drama is
the last great bubble to be burst. All the accepted authorities – your mother and
the other girls at your school, those sensational biology lessons that went into
such detail about the romantic lives of rabbits – will fill you in on the techni-
cal details of who puts what where. Erotic literature and those soft-focus,
passion-scorched films will prepare you for the hearts and flowers and the sweet
sighs of ecstasy. But who warns you about all the dribbles, the piggy grunts, the
embarrassing sound effects or the slimy wet patches on the duvet?

Frankly, when I embarked on my first relationship, all this came as a terrible shock to me. For instance, the realisation that what goes up must come down. Old sperm has a terrible habit of leaking into your underwear at the least convenient times, and making you smell like a fleet of herring trawlers. And while we're on smells, forget the subtle, musky odours so beloved of romantic novelists. We're talking about armpits and feet, reeking as their owners go into hormonal overdrive. I was disappointed, but I would have died rather than confess it. Being 'good at sex' was the duty of every liberated woman, and I didn't want my friends to think I was frigid. Besides, there was always the shaming possibility that I was doing something wrong.

'Sex has to be learned, like driving a car,' declares my friend Barbara, who has just removed her L-plates and announced her engagement. 'I'm 25 now, and I can honestly say that I didn't really enjoy sex at all until I met Ian. In my last two relationships, I now see that I was kidding myself – I was really just putting up with it instead of loving it.'

> '*Nobody takes you aside in advance to explain that an erect penis looks like a dachshund attached to a couple of mouldy prunes.*'

The truth is that most of us have 'put up with' sex at least once. It usually means lying resignedly on a bed and vibrating like a jelly being whacked with a spoon while some man you know enjoys an entirely private party on top of you. Where is the magic, and how do you find it?

Barbara laughs (and groans) when she looks back over her learning process. 'Losing my virginity – oh God, I still cringe. It was the classic thing of leaving home, aged eighteen, to go off to college. I thought that I was already quite a woman of the world. I had read piles of rude novels and, thanks to my biology A level, I could draw a cross section of an ovary with my eyes shut. But when I finally found myself on the rug in front of my gas fire with a real live boy – well, Judith Krantz it was not. It didn't hurt or anything, but all I could remember afterwards were the red elastic marks on his moony-white bottom.'

Louise, who's aged 23 and currently single, is also less than dewy-eyed about her formative sexual experiences. 'I wasn't much of a success at first because I couldn't look at a willy without laughing. And that's about the worst thing you can possibly do to a man, isn't it? Like laughing at the Union Jack on

Remembrance Day.' But who can blame her? Nobody ever thinks to take you aside in advance to explain that an erect penis looks like a dachshund attached to a couple of mouldy prunes. You must admit, however, that that little pink face, peering at your over the waistband of a pair of Y-fronts, can be a hilarious sight to the unprepared.

'I think I giggled,' Louise continues, 'because I felt uninvolved in some way. It's far simpler for men – either they're turned on or they're not. I didn't know then exactly how to get turned on. I just waited for something magical to happen. And until it did, I seemed to be standing aside from it all and observing the scene from a great distance. When you are in that frame of mind, you're quick to spot absurdities.

'Once I went to bed with a man who wanted to have sex in bizarre positions – he had me kneeling on a coffee table, while he came in from behind. The trouble was that I could see us in the mirror and we looked so undignified that I could hardly keep a straight face.'

Yes, when you start getting acrobatic, you can kiss your dignity goodbye. Doing it doggy-fashion, or standing up squashed against the wall, or boldly indulging in the slurping duet of the adventurous *soixante-neuf* can be huge fun, but noticeably short on aesthetic appeal.

However, simple nerves could have been another reason for Louise's fits of giggles. In our society, there are all kinds of opportunities for men to find out what the female body looks like without clothes. They have only to open a tabloid newspaper, or stroll around an art gallery ogling the lush Victorian nudes. But it's a different matter if we want to find out what a nude man looks like. Male genitals are kept as secret as the Queen's private telephone number.

Anna, aged 28, married for three years, feels that the shock of discovering that sex can be gross as well as gorgeous could even be considered a feminist issue: 'Look at the way boys are prepared for sex – everything they see and read sends out the message that women are these passive pieces of meat. Meanwhile, girls are getting insidious signals from a load of pretty-pink romantic tosh. We're led to believe that being folded into a pair of muscular arms is the be-all and end-all of our whole existence, while being earthy and rude and demanding is still considered "unfeminine". Nobody ever spoils the illusion by warning you beforehand to take along a hell of a lot of tissues.'

You develop quite a relationship with tissues over the years. Without wanting to put anyone off, I can reveal that routine marital sex often means waving a long strip of lavatory paper when you come to bed as a kind of mating signal. New-minted sperm is like wallpaper paste, and would you smear that all over your sheets? And as for old sperm, well, I won't linger over descriptions of those stiffly crusted tissues of the morning after.

Contraception is another great unsung turn-off. These days, single women need their heads examined if they don't embark on dates well armed with condoms. But even in the fabled days before such protection was necessary, barrier contraceptions were a huge source of comedy. 'One of my boyfriends,' remembers Helen, 'dropped a used condom on the bedroom floor. When I got up later, I slipped on it and sat down so hard, my eyes watered. It was the classic banana-skin routine. And I'll never forget the sight of my husband answering the phone, having been interrupted right in the middle of sex, standing there all serious, with the condom gently loosening round his shrinking willy.'

'My diaphragm is now a trusted friend,' says Anna, 'but the first time I used it, it kept zooming out of my fingers and hitting the bathroom walls. I ended up covered in spermicidal cream.'

Not an encouraging picture. But – and this is the essential 'but' – ask Anna, me or any of these women whether they feel that they have got the hang of good sex now, and the answer is a loud 'Yes'. The embarrassments and the disappointments will usually spring from being unused to physical intimacy with another person – possibly a person you're not too sure you want to be intimate with.

All the romantic propaganda lulls women into the belief that passion is a chemical reaction that can be switched on at will. In reality, it's a fickle and unpredictable phenomenon. You cherish tasteful dreams about your ideal man and what you will do with him when you meet him, and dutifully search for the kind of chaps who fit that fantasy identikit. Then, like a bolt of lightning, you find yourself turning hot and cold at the mere thought of someone who is not your chosen type at all. And, when that happens, you forget all about prudery, modesty and fastidiousness.

'When I met Ian,' Barbara says, 'I suddenly discovered what all the films and songs were about. I fancied him passionately and the physical intimacy of sex didn't seem at all embarrassing, but completely blissful. My mum had been burbling on for years about sex being right when you found True Love, and I always dismissed it as a cliché. But clichés are often based on truth.'

When you really, really fancy someone, the squelchy, sweaty, smelly details will just pale into insignificance. All you can think of is your own private, personal version of the sexy books you have read. And, in your opinion, the red-hot lovers in those are actually pretty weedy compared to the tiger you've got under your own duvet.

As Louise says, 'It isn't something you can explain. You just have to experience the magic for yourself.' The fairy tales about sex being hygienic, soft-focus and dainty are just that – fairy tales. But the part the brothers Grimm left out, about what the Prince and Princess got up to *while* they were living happily ever after – well, that's the part of the fairy tale that can come true. After all, when real romance enters the picture, what are a few squelches and grunts between great lovers?   ■

'I had sex with my boss for a pay rise.'

When sales manager, Sally, 28, went for a
promotion, she treated her boss to a
very special interview technique …
As told to **Natalie Dye**
March 2002

I've always been ambitious and competitive. I have to win at everything – board games, sports, work projects. So when a promotion came up at my firm, I knew the £6,000 pay rise had to be mine. Unfortunately, two other managers in my department had the same idea. There would be a board interview, but Steve, as group manager, would have the final say.

I spent the next month working long hours and trying to wow Steve, but it was obvious that the race for that promotion was still wide open. I had to think of a way to make Steve choose me.

Steve was in his early 40s, married with kids, and good-looking with a nice body and cute smile. He didn't flirt, but I'd seen a spark in his bright blue eyes when he interviewed me. I knew he wanted me. Maybe it was the way he held eye contact with me that bit too long. Maybe it was because he seemed slightly jittery around me. I sensed a sexual vibe, and when it came to that promotion, I was determined to use it.

I had it all planned out. I'd seduce Steve, get him back to my place and have sex. He'd be so worried I'd tell his wife, he'd give me the job to shut me up. I wouldn't really tell her – I didn't want to split up a family. But I was happy for him to think I would. The way I saw it, I deserved the job. It's not as though I was jumping over better candidates. This was just an insurance policy.

I chose a week when I was working closely with Steve on a new project. I'm always smartly dressed, but I added a few subtle touches – a lower-cut top, shorter skirts, expensive perfume, wearing my hair long instead of tied back. I arrived early each morning and worked late, but getting Steve on his own was proving to be very tricky. Monday passed, then Tuesday and Wednesday. I started to panic. My interview was the following Monday – I was running out of time.

On Friday, Steve asked me to put together a summary of our project so far. I'd finished it by mid-afternoon, but stayed at my computer, poring over it, until Steve and I were the only ones left. Even though I wanted sex with him purely for that promotion, I'd started to get turned on by the challenge. The idea of ruthlessly bedding a man for money was really erotic, and the more I thought about it, the hornier I became. I felt myself getting aroused at my desk. Each time I looked at Steve I got a real aching between my legs.

> 'We kissed each other hard, and from there it was fast and furious.'

I sidled over to his desk, carrying the report. 'Do you fancy going through it in the pub?', I asked. He gave me an undeniably sexy look, and said, 'There's some wine in the boardroom. Why don't we go there?'. So I followed him, massively turned on. The boardroom had no interior windows – and a lockable door. Did Steve have the same idea as me? I told myself I was imagining things, but the way he'd taken the lead made me feel really horny. Neither of us said a word until we got there. He closed the door behind us and locked it, saying, 'We don't want the cleaners coming in, do we?'. I couldn't believe how easy this was going to be.

Steve poured the wine. He'd created the chance, now all I had to do was go for it. I gave him a sexy grin and said, 'No-one knows we're up here, do they? We could do anything'. I ran my fingers up the inside of his thigh, over his huge erection and up his chest. Steve moaned as I touched him.

We kissed each other hard, and from there it was fast and furious. I slid my hand inside his trousers while Steve tore open my blouse and kissed and stroked my breasts. He was rough but skilful. I almost orgasmed under his touch, but he wanted to satisfy himself first. He guided my head down to his crotch, so I dropped to my knees, and took his penis in my mouth. As I sucked him, Steve became very vocal, talking dirty and begging me not to stop until he came in my mouth.

I was so close to orgasm – I stood up, pulled my knickers aside and started to masturbate myself. Steve thrust his fingers inside me, probing hard. Sensing I was about to come, he lifted me up onto the board table, parted my legs and pressed his tongue against my clitoris. I came within seconds.

Steve quickly pulled his trousers up while I did up my blouse. I was amazed how turned on I'd been – what had started out as a ploy to land a job had ended up with great sex. Steve said, 'We'd better keep this to ourselves – you don't want anyone thinking you got the job because you give great head!' I grinned. That was fine by me. I went home and masturbated over our encounter.

At the interview I was confident and relaxed. I was convinced the job was mine, I'd even decided what I was going to do with the money. Three days later, the MD called me up to the boardroom. There, standing on the spot where I'd brought Steve to climax, I was told the job had been given to Miranda, a plain, married graduate.

Back in the office I was so furious. Steve came over and said he was sorry I hadn't been successful. I didn't even look up at him. I didn't regret what I did – it was amazing – and I certainly wasn't ashamed, but I was absolutely gutted that my plan hadn't worked. I hated to fail. I started looking for a better job, and within a month had found one. I don't hold a grudge against Steve – I'd engineered the whole thing and he went for it. Who can blame him? ■

Names and details have been changed.

CHAPTER 3

LIPSTICK FEMINISM

Writing in *Cosmopolitan* in 1983, Erin Pizzey, renowned as a feminist and champion of battered women, said 'I remember hiding my copies of *Cosmopolitan* in the cupboard because I was involved in the women's movement, which was born in Britain at the same time as the magazine.'

Feminism and *Cosmopolitan* were never easy bedfellows, at least not as far as the radicals within the women's liberation movement were concerned. Erin went on to say: 'Like any newly found group of religious zealots, the women's movement disapproved loudly, and those of us who were unfaithful to the cause had surreptitious meetings on how to seduce a man *Cosmo*-style. Subsequently, of course, *Cosmo* helped to publicise most of the tenets of the women's movement: knowledge of abortion, contraception, equal opportunity, women in Parliament, job opportunities. All these issues and many more became readily available to all women in a readable form, thanks to this healthy coalition between a magazine and a movement.

Journalist and feminist author Joan Smith, writing in the *Independent* about the 30th anniversary of *Cosmopolitan*, in February 2002, expressed similar sentiments: 'I loved *Cosmo*, devouring it with the same enthusiasm as I felt for

Simone de Beauvoir

The Second Sex (1949)

This work firmly established Simone de Beauvoir as a philosophical and political leader. The roots of 'gender studies', were born in 1949 with the publication of The Second Sex. *De Beauvoir claimed that woman's traditional destiny accounted for her subordination to man; women are inferior to men only because they are made so: 'One is not born, but rather becomes, a woman.'*

Betty Friedan

The Feminine Mystique (1963)

Friedan argued that women as a class suffer a variety of forms of discrimination, and attacked the notion that women can find fulfilment only through childbearing and home-making. She wrote about the feelings of worthlessness in women that result from being intellectually, economically, and emotionally dependent on one's husband. However, many people were unwilling to admit that a 'feminine mystique' existed, and Friedan's agent and publishers thought most men and women would feel threatened by the book's main idea. Once published, the book became one of the most talked-about and controversial books of the ▶

The Female Eunuch. I was a teenage reader of *Cicero* and *Jackie*, T S Eliot and Georgette Heyer; so I wasn't at all discomfited to find Nobel prize-winning novelists and male pin-ups in the same magazine'. But in the eyes of the movement, our attitude towards men was precisely the problem. We never fully engaged in the battle of the sexes; passionate skirmishes were more *Cosmo's* style. We criticised men – big-time – and we got angry at their entrenched attitudes and sometimes boorish behaviour. We loathed men who wouldn't listen and the ones who put us down. And all those who regarded women merely as 'sport'. We abhorred the bosses who patronised us at work and the others who tried to put their hands up our skirts. We were appalled by physical violence of any kind and, of course, by men who raped. And we were almost as appalled by the male judges who assumed that women who dressed provocatively or went out at late at night were simply 'asking for it'. But we didn't regard *all* men as rapists. And we didn't regard all men as the enemy. We also wore lipstick

Paradoxically, if the women's movement saw *Cosmo* as traitor to the cause for pandering to men, there were plenty of others – yes, mostly men – who regarded us as firebrand feminists. If you disapproved of men in any way you were probably 'too ugly to get one' or a 'loony lesbian'.

Cosmo readers did tend to be feminists, even if the word sometimes got stuck in their throats and it was hard for them to admit. Feminists didn't exactly get a good press. Feminists, as portrayed in the media, were man-hating harridans with nothing better to do than burn their bras and examine their clitorises at consciousness-raising workshops. Who wants to be saddled with that kind of label? I remember a rather smart dinner party in the early seventies at which I explained to the man sitting next to me that I worked on *Cosmopolitan*. He responded, 'But you seem far too nice to be one of those ghastly feminists.' I smiled sweetly, pouted prettily and then launched into my lecture on what we women had to put up with, including men like him. Needless to say, I was never placed next to that particular man at a dinner party again.

Six decades before *Cosmo* was born, the writer Rebecca West provided a clue to society's attitude to feminism. Writing in the year 1913, she said 'I myself have never been able to find out what precisely feminism is ... I only know that people call me a feminist whenever I express sentiments that differentiate me from a doormat or a prostitute.' Even when the official women's liberation movement was launched in the 1960s, much the same attitudes towards feminism prevailed.

For *Cosmopolitan*, feminism had many strands. We wanted to change the laws and we wanted to change attitudes. There was the issue of equality, of course – equality of opportunity, equality of pay - and freedom from sexual discrimination. But our feminist philosophy also encompassed sexual liberation – the freedom to make our own decisions about our sex lives, to say 'yes' without being labelled a slag or a slut, to say 'no' without being labelled as frigid. Sexual assertiveness was always on our feminist agenda, empowering women to explore the nature of their sexuality without shame, and to claim – as well as to give – sexual pleasure. And as much as anything else feminism was about finding a route to self-confidence, to a genuine belief in oneself as having equal value in a still male-dominated society.

Becoming the same as men was never on our wish-list. We didn't want to *be* like men, we just wanted access to some of their advantages, and to demonstrate that most of what they could do, we could do, too – and sometimes rather better. Who, in their right mind, could possibly argue with that?

As the stories that follow demonstrate, when *Cosmo* launched it was tentative in its approach to feminism, unwilling to align itself too emphatically, particularly with the more extreme wings of the movement. Gillian Tindall's article for *Cosmopolitan* in 1973 decries the feminists for lacking a sense of humour, while grudgingly acknowledging the movement's 'useful functions'. The following year novelist Margaret Drabble paved the way for solidarity with a piece about the joys of female friendship and how women can be supportive of one another … a warm and sisterly piece which couldn't possibly frighten off the reader. In October 1980 Eileen Fairweather came across as far more feisty with the message, 'Liberation is too important to leave to the feminists.' This time the tone was sharper, less compromising, and paved the way for the more forthright feminism of *Cosmo* in the eighties and early nineties.

But as the nineties progressed and a new generation of younger women reached adulthood, entered the job market, and embarked on relationships with a generation of young men who were markedly less chauvinist than the one which preceded them, feminism was bound to take a different form. The

decade, and led to Friedan being called the 'mother' of the feminist movement.

Germaine Greer
The Female Eunuch (1970)

In this bestselling book Greer claimed that women are neutralised, essentially sexless, within patriarchy. She criticised the mechanisms of the traditional nuclear family and advocated a revolutionary empowerment of women. This book portrayed marriage as a legalised form of slavery for women, and attacked the denial and misrepresentation of female sexuality by a male-dominated society.

Kate Millett
Sexual Politics (1970)

Kate Millett's main question throughout this book was whether the relationship between the sexes can be political. She demonstrated how patriarchy's attitudes and systems penetrate literature, philosophy, psychology, and politics, and proposed a sexual revolution that would 'bring the institution of patriarchy to an end'. The book caused a storm when it was published, rocking the foundations of the literary canon by castigating classics such as D H Lawrence's Lady Chatterley's Lover *and Norman Mailer's* The ▶

Naked and the Dead, *for their use of sex to degrade and undermine women. It also attacked the very people credited as authors of sexual liberation, such as Freud and Henry Miller.*

Marilyn French
The Women's Room
(1977)

This is the haunting story of Mira Ward, a fifties wife who becomes a woman of the seventies. From the shallow excitement of cocktail parties and casual affairs, to the varied nightmares of rape, madness and loneliness, her experiences represent the dawning awareness of the exhilaration of liberation. Mira rebuilds her life after divorce and finds men incidental – there is no co-existence between the sexes. The novel was a bestseller. ∎

polemical pieces became less frequent, to be replaced by pithy reminders that there was still a way to go. Articles like, 'You know you're a feminist when …' written in 1993, kept the issues alive in an entertaining and more palatable for a new wave of readers who'd grown up assuming – and expecting – equality.

The story 'Feminists Who Strip', written by Melissa Benn in 1995, served as a Requiem on the subject of feminism. After the departure of Marcelle d'Argy Smith as editor in 1995, the subject was never again broached, other than in special *Cosmo* retrospectives, such as an important anniversary of the magazine.

As I reflect on how energising it was to be involved in feminism *Cosmo*-style in the seventies and eighties – how exciting it was to feel so much part of the drive to change women's lives for the better – I am aware of the danger of indulging in feminist nostalgia. For a new generation of editors, starting with Mandi Norwood and continuing with current editor Lorraine Candy, there is a belief that the tenets of feminism have been so well-absorbed into young women's psyches that direct discussion of the issues no longer seems relevant.

Of course if you were to look at where most of the real power – and the real money – is today, it would be easy to show that men still run the world, and that 'Girl Power' is no substitute. *Cosmopolitan*'s legacy is that at least it took the fear out of feminism. It gave women the confidence to be feminine *and* feminist. And it even made it seem like fun.

'The sex war is surely a game rather than a real battle ...'

The feminists are building a cage for themselves, warns **Gillian Tindall**
October 1973

Long ago, which is to say in 1968 before the Women's Liberation Movement was invented, I wrote in an article that it was unfair that my photo had to show me as young and good humoured while a male contributor could get away with looking old and cross. It wasn't intended as a serious complaint. I have always felt that a woman's life has its advantages as well as disadvantages – and I do mean profound, worthwhile advantages, nothing to do with the use of 'feminine wiles'.

It had never struck me that being treated as a sex object was a grudge to be taken to heart. Most of the men who talk in public about women as 'birds', or whistle after them in the street, seem to me to be putting on a jokey, defensive act, and to be secretly rather awed by female skills such as having babies. The 'Sex War' is surely a game, a jousting match rather than a real battle, a metaphor for sexual intercourse with the male in the role of the aggressor and the woman in the role of the injured party? As I say, a bit of a joke.

I was taken aback to receive letters from women who had taken my article seriously. They wrote 'how bitterly I agree with you,' or hectored me on how I must 'liberate myself from male domination'. That phrase has become endlessly familiar since, but *then* it was quite new.

Some of the letters aired genuine grievances such as job discrimination, deserting husbands, etc, but most made an unwarranted jump from the particular to the general, from 'this is unfair' to 'society is unfair,' from 'I suffer' to 'women suffer.'

Other letters came from obvious man-haters, all spleen and insistence that masturbation is nicer anyway. Others again came from people for whom the complication of being feminine seemed to be just one more factor in their all-round inadequacy or neurosis. These particular people would, I suspected, have been just as badly off had they been men – possibly worse, since society expects quite a lot from men.

> 'You are no sisters of mine, and *I* find *you* oppressive.'

I had unwittingly uncovered emotions, needs, resentments. The fact that I was basically unsympathetic to them did not abolish them; to the sufferer the problems were real, and anyone has a right to air their personal grievances, but *as* personal viewpoints, not as sweeping pronouncements on society and womanhood!

This is what repelled me about those letters, what continued to repel me when, a year later, what I had stumbled on accidentally, reared its head as Women's Lib.

Alien women – alien *people* – band together by all means, have your meetings, your 'consciousness-raising groups,' comfort and support each other – but don't, please, claim to speak for womanhood in general and certainly not for the likes of me. You are no sisters of mine, and *I* find *you* oppressive.

Six years ago I didn't have to dissociate myself publicly from nuts and wets just because they happened to be the same sex as me: now I do, for some sort of moral glow has attached itself to the movement. Enlightened people – or those who wish to be thought enlightened – feel that Women's Lib must be vaguely a Good Thing, like democracy or free milk, however much they may shy away from the lunatic excess of SCUM (Society for Cutting Up Men). Certain journalists who owe their jobs to the fact that they are women claim fashionable Libbish affiliations. Perfectly sensible men seem to feel that, in order not to be classed as male chauvinists, they have to make respectful genuflections in the same direction.

It is not hard to see where the pressure comes from. Like other ideologies – Marxism, evangelical Christianity, vegetarianism – Women's Liberation adopts the unanswerable moral line that only *they* have seen the light and that those who disagree with them are still blind. Their convictions are genuine. So are the convictions of those who believe that the earth is flat, that animal fats are poison or that God is angry. Conviction is no guide to truth.

If 'freedom to be yourself' means anything, it surely means being an individual with other interests, identities and capacities beyond your gender? Yet far from liberating women from the label 'feminine', the movement has pinned it more obviously and firmly on them. It has encouraged them to huddle together in defensive, exclusive groups to which men are rarely admitted. 'I'm right into Women's Lib,' said one girl to me, 'I give all my time to it.' Goodness, what a free, varied life!

The minority of men who really do despise women have a better excuse to do so than ever before, for some of the sisters are the worst possible advertisements for their movement. Unattractive just as *people*, they appear to have aped the worst of male characteristics – aggressiveness, pomposity, coarseness – rather than the best.

While I would not deny that there are specific injustices against women in our society, mainly financial, which could and should be rectified, campaigning about them is only a tiny part of the Women's Lib scene. What seems to appeal to many women is the cult-aspect of the movement, the whole idea of a sisterhood and of man as the oppressor, which goes far beyond specific instances of discrimination – 'The institution for oppressing females is marriage, and this institution exists for the purpose of extorting domestic and personal service, including production and care of offspring, who become subordinates of the male-supremist state.' The vocabulary is not always as paranoid as this, but it betrays the nature of the fantasy.

Women, far from being encouraged to see their troubles in a wide social perspective, are urged to exaggerate them, sometimes grotesquely, as when mere ogling by men is described as 'visual rape'. Some Libbers seem to have a virtual obsession about rape and wife-beating, things which, while they do exist, are not part of the real-life experience of most women here and now.

My guess is that many women have simply exchanged domination by a man for domination by an idea. One woman even published an article recently in which she explained that she sold herself to men in order to raise money for the movement. This traditional, self-abasing female pastime, and pseudo-selfless justification, has nothing to do with freedom.

Do such postures really matter? Perhaps not. Where, however, the cult becomes offensive is where grandiose comparisons are used to give stature to trivial situations. The white, Western twentieth-century woman who compares her lot with that of a Negro slave is not showing 'radical insight', but merely that she does not know what she is talking about. If she did, she would not have the nerve to try to elevate her own luxury grudges to the level of real suffering, real dehumanising deprivation. Similarly offensive is the tendency to denigrate the real satisfactions inherent for both sexes in love and commitment with children seen as a sort of enemy who can only be contained by '24-hour nurseries.'

This said, one should add that the movement does perform useful functions. Its very existence proves that it, or something, is needed by many women – though I wish that the need could be provided by some cult more apt to promote genuine self-responsibility rather than one which encourages the childish belief that life ought to be perfect and it's someone else's fault if it isn't.

At the sane end of the Women's Lib spectrum, more than one woman has said to me that the movement has made her get to know herself better; fair enough, any road to self-knowledge has something to be said for it. Others have spoken of their groups as places for finding feminine friends, having intense discussions without a man present, a supportive group in times of trouble, a potential pressure group.

Very useful, I agree: something like the Women's Institute, only anti jam-making instead of pro? (I like jam-making myself, but I will defend to the death anyone's right not to make it.) No, no, they said crossly, not at *all* like. I have yet to be convinced. ■

Why I like women

Who says women are incapable of solidarity? Who says
women in groups are dreary and joyless? Novelist
Margaret Drabble believes we are loyal, tolerant,
discreet and we need each other more than
ever in these days of militant feminism ...
February 1974

There was once a widely held view that women didn't like
other women. They were supposed to be jealous of one another, petty,
malicious, eaten up with rivalry. Given an opportunity, they would betray their
best friends, and would always speak unkindly of one another in private.

Upholders of this view would point to the fact that women seem incapable
of solidarity – they don't join trade unions, they don't fight for their rights, not
only because they aren't aggressive enough, but because they don't like one
another enough to spend sufficient time together to get organised. Women who
did like other women were thought of as faintly ridiculous, and women's groups
were labelled as stuffy, sexless, parochial and silly by all those who didn't go to
them. It wasn't only men who criticised, either.

I well remember being told, when I was at university in an all-women's college, that I should use the university library and not the college library, because
the college library was stuffy and spinstery and chintzy. (I don't remember if it
had chintz curtains, but it may have done once.) I was told this by a very attractive, sexy young don, who was always much admired by her male students. I was
slightly outraged by her remarks, though at the time, being about eighteen, I

was very keen to prove myself on the side of the young and swinging, so off I would plod to the sexy masculine university library with its huge phallic tower, and struggle with endless floors of books, and lifts, and catalogues, and tiresome men who wanted or didn't want to have coffee with me, instead of getting the books much more conveniently out of the library down the corridor.

The don's view is now I think as outdated as those chintz curtains themselves. We can now openly admit that we like the company of other women. I don't think it at all clever not to, and very cowardly to pretend not to when one does. I've always liked women, which is lucky for me as I've known plenty of them.

I was brought up in a largely female household between two sisters. With my father away at war for the first years of my childhood, I suppose I was imbued with the idea that the female way of doing things was the norm rather than an inferior deviation, which must be the impression received by girls in many households, particularly where there are dominating brothers. (I do have a brother, but he is much younger than I, and when he was little I always felt rather maternal towards him – I probably looked it too. I remember going to collect him from school one day, and when he claimed me as his sister, one of his friends said to him very firmly: 'That's not a sister, that's an *aunt*.') So I grew up with the idea that women are all right – that they can be taken seriously, educated, that they can win prizes and get good jobs.

I also went to a girls' boarding school, which I must confess to having enjoyed. I was lucky in finding myself with an exceptionally good group of friends, but I think I would have enjoyed it anyway, as I was gregarious and obsequious by nature, and very good at getting away with or concealing the crimes I chose to commit. I didn't find it oppressive living with so many girls – in fact I enjoyed the slightly hot-house atmosphere of romantic curiosity that filled our long late-night conversations about sex and men. It probably wasn't very good for us: we were encouraged to think of men as violent, unpredictable creatures with animal passions and no self-control, which is clearly not a good idea for girls to acquire. It made those of us who suspected we, too, were violent, unpredictable creatures with no self-control, feel guilty and unnatural. But I didn't object to the girls. I liked girls. They were good company.

I liked, too, being in a women's college. Of course, there wasn't much choice in my day, for nearly all colleges that took women were single sex, and the thought of men and women sharing a flat was almost unknown to the authorities. Perhaps there was something wrong with me, but at that stage I had little desire to live in a free-for-all situation where men could stay all night in my room whenever they fancied. I was quite happy to wave goodbye to them (most of them) at midnight. I often wish these days that a loud bell would ring at midnight, and enable me to say I had to go to bed at once in my solitary bed, a wish shared by many women of my acquaintance, though some are too polite to admit it.

Living in institutions is most unfashionable these days among the young – happily so for the authorities, as there aren't nearly enough institutions to go round – and single sex institutions are very much outmoded. But I had nothing against it at all. I liked it. I liked the austere, hard-working suffragette inheritance of the women's colleges, and the thought of that long line of courageous, dedicated women stretching behind me gave me a great deal of strength. Nowadays, when I go into the British Museum to use the reading room, I get the same sense of satisfaction when I find myself labelled as a Lady Reader. It seems a perfectly acceptable destiny, to be a Lady Reader.

'I enjoyed the slightly hot-house atmosphere of romantic curiosity that filled our long late-night conversations about sex and men.'

When I left college and married, my feelings towards my fellow sisters (I like the use of the word 'sisters' and was delighted the first time I received a letter signed 'Yours in sisterhood') I underwent a certain crisis. In a sense I am still struggling with it. For it is at this point that the dividing of the ways takes place.

Until marriage, most women get on well enough, with much genuine liking and some conspiratorial sense of communal interest; after it, attitudes harden, malice and envy set in, despair and separation and triumph and secrecy take over. Girls are obliged by sulky anti-social husbands to cast off their best friends, or to meet them secretly for furtive hurried lunches. Women start to boast about the numbers of their babies or their possessions. Career women stare in contempt at the dirty carpets and milk-stained skirts of their once-fashionable baby-ridden friends. Young mothers go home from parties to weep bitterly because nobody asked them about anything but the baby, while at the same time they know that in their hearts they are not really interested in talking about anything but the baby.

It is at this stage that women do their best to behave as badly as they are traditionally supposed to towards one another – they try, deliberately, to instil envy and fear in those who have chosen differently from themselves, they try to bolster up their own confidence by destroying that of their friends. Or that is how it used to be. Perhaps it is getting better. The correspondence columns of newspapers and magazines used to be full of the career–motherhood debate. Nowadays it seems less conspicuous, perhaps as women realise that it is possible to do both, or either, and still be regarded as a 'real woman'.

A more open society, and a greater frankness on the part of women themselves, has made it impossible to regard all career women as hard, ambitious, sexless bitches. It is equally obvious now, as it wasn't ten years ago, that not all women with children are empty-headed morons fit for nothing but baby talk and the kitchen sink.

I still remember with some pain the problems that this particular phase in my own life caused me. I married young and had my children young, and I was deeply involved in the whole process, somewhat to my surprise; but at the same time, I didn't want to be thought of as a mere wife, or a mere mother. I had got the idea (not from home, it is true – it must have crept in later) that men were somehow more interesting than women, and that they talked about more interesting things. So, whenever I went out, half of me would want to talk about books and politics and so forth, partly because I was genuinely interested in them, and partly because I wanted to prove I hadn't turned into a cabbage; while the other half was absolutely longing to talk to the other mothers present about the difficulties of getting enough sleep, the advisability of getting solid food at an early age, the symptoms of various childhood diseases and children's ailments and the cost of disposable nappies.

There was a real conflict between the two interests, or so I thought at the time. No *intelligent* person could join the women's conversation. Why then did I find it so interesting? Had my brain really rotted as so many books seemed to imply it would?

The mistake lay, of course, in my accepting the man–woman, intelligent–stupid dichotomy at all. If one undervalues the interests of women, then, of course, one must become a traitor and a woman-hater. But there is no need to do so, and nowadays I can find myself quite honestly admitting that sometimes

I prefer to talk about children, or cooking, or shoes, than about inflation, or immigration, or population. It all depends who is doing the talking. One can hear a lot of boring nonsense about inflation, and some very fascinating realities about children. And the fact that men find some women's talk dull in no way diminishes its value. Women, on the whole, find talk about racing cars dull.

It is largely men who have put about the idea that women do not get on with one another, and that any really aspiring woman ought to want to be a man and stay on to drink port after dinner. In plays and novels written by men, we see women quarrelling, usually over a man. Even women have tended to adopt some of the same conventions except for the superbly confident Jane Austen, who allows her silly characters to be silly, be they of either sex, and her sensible characters to be sensible. Shakespeare is full of silly women. But recently things have changed, and women have started to describe female friendships and loyalties as they really are.

There are large areas of life in which women get on well together, and need one another's support – not only in personal friendships, which always existed however the novelists have neglected them, but also at work, as neighbours, as mothers. Working and non-working mothers can usually rely on a network of friends who will help out in a crisis, or even on a regular basis of exchange. I haven't noticed that men, for all their clubmanship and comradeship, are particularly good at sharing their cars to give one another lifts to work, where-as women in all parts of society are good at organising baby-minding and child-collecting systems.

In some ways, women have come to need one another more than they ever did. Most women used to rely on their mothers for advice about sex and babies, but so many of them now live so far from their mothers and, anyway, the advice is so quickly out of date in a changing world, that they have to turn to their own age groups. I can't be alone in having found myself one or two substitute mothers – not as old as my real mother, but closer at hand, and older than I – who give me, often unsolicited, much of the information that I need about such practical and psychological matters that are new to me, such as receding gums, teenage children, reluctance to work. I am aware that I fulfil the same role for others younger than myself. It's a chain, a continuity. If one didn't like talking to women, how much of it one would miss. One would also miss the pleasure of gossip, a pleasure which has been constantly derided because it is so extraordinarily basic and agreeable.

Women have a genius for gossip. It is much underrated. Men often assert that women in groups are dreary and joyless, whereas men in clubs are jolly, witty, gregarious, and the proper envy of women. At the same time, men condemn women for gossiping. They do not seem to realise that much gossip is profound, joyful, creative and witty, and that where two or three women are gathered together, in a back yard, launderette, tea shop or drawing room, they are as likely as not to be engaged in an extremely satisfying occupation. Jane Austen, again, understood this perfectly, and her characters frequently engage in intense and fascinating discussions of neighbours, clothes and marriages which are as absorbing now as they were when they were written.

The art of small talk, of making something out of nothing, of making common ground out of uttermost disparity, is on the whole a woman's art. I saw this act embodied, recently, in a public ward in a women's hospital. There lay twelve women, from completely different walks of life, suffering from a not very wide range of women's complaints. The experience itself had perhaps been common ground, but the women improved on it immensely. They had brought photographs, they had their own little possessions – books, cards, knitting, magazines, flowers. And all day long they chatted, exchanging stories, comparing nightdresses, discussing not only their operations but also their jobs, their marriages, their houses. No lasting friendships were formed, and there was, it is true, one flash of malice. One woman was a little too insistent on the grandeur of her daughter's approaching wedding, which went down badly with an overworked, divorced young mother. But the achievement was considerable.

I was even more impressed by it when I went, a month or two later, on several occasions to see a friend in a men's ward in another hospital. There, the atmosphere was completely different. Where the women had made little homes for themselves out of one or two possessions, the men were content to lie in their institution beds by their institution tables. They looked miserable and bored. Nobody spoke to anybody else – there was none of the small interchange, the supportive comparing of notes. When one man groaned in pain, my friend told me, the others swore at him, and left him to it. Instead of a valiant effort to make the best of things, there was apathy, self-neglect and hostility. And it could not be explained away by saying that the men were more seriously ill, for one of the most lively of the women was clearly in a bad way. She had a frilly hair net, which she would put on at night with great aplomb and many jokes. She was old, frail, and alone in the world, and very amusing.

I am also greatly impressed by how nice the women who come to my adult education classes are to one another. The classes are open to both sexes, but as they are during the day, all the students but one are women – some of them are young mothers who leave their babies in the crèche, some are women with grown families off their hands and some are retired professional people. Again, they come from very different backgrounds and, again, they have a most impressive ability for finding common ground. They are responsive to one another's problems, interested in one another, discreet and tolerant.

As a group, I like to think we show none of the weaknesses that are associated with the female sex – we are not petty, malicious, or silly; we are not lazy and we do not compete with one another. It is true that we tend to digress, but I see this as a virtue. It is also true that over coffee we are as likely to discuss sick children as Ibsen and D H Lawrence but, again, I see this as a virtue.

'Women have a genius for gossip. It is much underrated. Men condemn women for gossiping. They do not realise that much gossip is profound, joyful, witty.'

I hope that this article will not be taken as an attack on men. I like men, too. I like mixed gatherings, though I no longer feel the need to prove myself by talking to men, not women. (What I do still dislike is finding myself a statutory woman in a group of men – an unnatural and uncomfortable role.) But I do, as I hope I've made clear, like women, too, and I think there is a place for their own groupings, and their own private relationships. I think that women in this country have become more confident in the last few years, and more able to assert themselves, and their own legitimate interests.

As Virginia Woolf said, why should war and football be regarded as important, and the buying of clothes as trivial? At the same time (and much as I like the idea of sisterhood) I don't like the new American notion that to be a proper woman (whatever that is) one must dislike men. Why? I would hate to see women's friendships reinterpreted by the old-fashioned masculine theory of lesbian conspiracy. Let us like one another, and leave it at that. ■

'Liberation is too important to leave to the feminists.'

Yelling 'I'm all right, Jill, pull up the ladder,' is neither sisterly nor wise. With unemployment hitting women harder than men, we must make sure we hold on to some equality.
Eileen Fairweather
October 1980

My stock response to the inevitable 'Haw, haw, and have you burnt your bra?' is to look down at my 38D and reply that, if I did, I'd knock myself out running for the bus. After seven years' active involvement in the Women's Liberation movement I ought to be used to such comments from men, but telling myself that men of quality aren't threatened by women who want equality doesn't always console me. Making the effort patiently to explain the real issues of feminism does sometimes pay off, but there are still men who prefer to believe that all 'Libbers' are mad, bad, or just plain ugly.

Rather than risk being on the receiving end of such put-downs, many women still preface their commitment to equality with the apologetic, 'I'm not into women's lib … but …' Lamely they explain that they do, after all, like having men open doors. They're probably as aware as the next sister that, for every door men open, there are ten others they'll cheerfully slam in your face. None of us *really* believes that our frail, feminine wrists will crack at the sight of a doorknob, but playing grateful for sex-war consolation prizes does, at least, mean you avoid the Loony Feminist label.

I was terrified of that label too, so when I went to my first-ever Women's Liberation meeting, back in 1972, I wore elaborate make-up, clinging clothes, five-inch heels, and took along a boyfriend as protection. No way did I want anyone sneering that *I* was only interested because something was wrong with my hormones.

I went along because, at eighteen, I'd only recently made the shocking discovery that women were even supposed to be inferior. I only had sisters, so never had to wait on brothers, my mother was a gutsy and no-frills lady and I'd gone to an all-girls' school. I was independent-minded, an extrovert, had a raucous sense of humour and thought that was a fairly OK way for a girl to be. Then I started dating boys and discovered that I'd got it all wrong. From the number of dates who never rang back, I gathered that striding along, cracking dirty jokes between explaining The Meaning of Life, wasn't quite what the teen magazines meant when they said 'just be yourself'.

So, instead, I'd belatedly learned to play chameleon, to agree with whatever a bloke said and automatically take his interests as mine. Football, sculpture, motorbikes or marine biology, between first meeting and first date I became an instant, if side-line, devotee of them all.

> '*Even if your man is a dedicated anti-sexist who knows all about clitorises, kids and washing up, private revolutions don't provide all the answers ...*'

The trouble was, I could never keep it up. Being redolent with mute mystique seemed to mean pretending I'd had a full-frontal lobotomy, and somehow that just didn't come naturally. As for staring adoringly up at that great manly jaw, it gave me a crick in the neck, not to mention bent ankles and a slouch if he was actually smaller than me. After five or six dates I'd forget to stoop, or titter, and would make the elementary mistake of being myself. So, once again, exit disgruntled Hero in search of a Real Woman.

To this day, I still joke that Jesus is the only man who ever really understood me. Growing up Catholic and female had, in fact, meant being constantly faced with contradictions. Long before sex equality was fashionable, the nuns at my convent grammar school took it for granted that 'their girls' could and even should, want to be career high-fliers. In chapel, though, it was back to a straight Vatican line on how the highest role for a woman was that of the mother. Once we married, our career aspirations would be limited to next year's baby. It seemed that only nuns, who topped the vocational tree, could expect to spend much time upright.

From being a devout Catholic I became, technically speaking, a heretic. For years now, I've been involved in campaigns that directly challenge the church, through seeking to defend and extend women's abortion rights. I've written articles in support of a woman's right to choose, addressed innumerable meetings, co-authored and acted in a play about abortion, demonstrated, plotted, and occasionally, out of sheer frustration and anger, cried.

Eighty-year-old women who endured the back street abortionist have come up to shake my hand, and men have thrown beer glasses. While I know that many anti-abortionists are sincere, I profoundly mistrust and resent the campaigning motives of a male-run religion which, as I know from the inside, is less pro-life than just anti-sex and anti-woman, and sees constant childbirth as women's punishment for being daughters of temptress Eve. As another rebellious Catholic once wrote on a Dublin toilet wall, Eve was *framed*.

My first consciousness-raising group taught me that it's not only Catholics who are trained in female shame and guilt. Jewish women have also got a double-dose: knowing that your brother's morning prayers include the delightful 'Thank God I was not born a woman' does a lot for a growing girl's pride. And whether we'd been religiously educated or not, all of us knew the price of straying from the ideal image of woman as virgin.

The sexual revolution was, in 1972, supposedly at its height, but many a hippy refuge had, painfully, discovered that men still saw sex as conquest – conquest without concessions, too, because cool chicks didn't ask for commitment but just 'went with the flow'. Then, if they became pregnant or jealous *he* went with the flow too, and found himself a new woman.

Nowadays, when so much of the feminist philosophy – at least so far as it affects personal life – has filtered through into public consciousness, it's difficult to convey the incredible excitement and sheer *relief* of those early days. Most of us had feared that, if we weren't too hot at this job of being a woman, let alone overjoyed by it, then that was just proof of our personal failure.

Now, through consciousness raising, conferences, and those high-as-a-kite midnight conversations, we could share the horror stories and the dreams and ambitions we'd buried for so long. The isolation barrier was broken; women were learning to be friends, and finding that our identity and worth didn't have to depend on men. Together, we could relinquish the role of victim.

Of course, the women's movement didn't invent sisterhood; women have always supported each other, together plotted survival. What feminism did do was bring female solidarity into the open. Proclaiming pride in and loyalty to one's own sex gave many women confidence and strength; but to others, it seemed, and often still does seem, either plain silly or a direct threat.

In any power system, it's inevitable that some will accept the ruling group's definition of those below and therefore play 'the happy slave'. Still others are so male-identified that they don't even like other women; they're the ones who are quicker than any man to condemn another woman as stupid, sexless or sluttish; the ones who act as patriarchy's crack-shot back-up squad, the inside agents who obligingly bitch other women back into line. In return, they receive approval from certain men – some reward! For I fail to see how you can look down on your own sex without despising yourself.

> 'Even having a batterer around the house accords status, as women who are divorced or single all know. Bachelor is not a term of derision; spinster is.'

You can give all your loyalty and respect to men, get off on pseudo-flattering songs about how 'You're more than a woman to me', yet at the end of the day you've still got those breasts and that tell-tale womb. When the boys make jokes about rape, it's still you they're sniggering at.

But maybe all this seems old hat ... you believe that everything's *different* now. In the eleven years since the present women's movement began, hasn't the sexual revolution been won? Why, then, keep carping?

Actually, I'd love to agree that feminism is just a dated seventies hobby, and was never more than the serious girl's alternative to disco-dancing and window-shopping. There are days when all I want to do with yet-another-petition is use it for scrap paper, nights when I'd love to be out painting the town red instead of sitting at a meeting getting a stiff bum. And I do 'switch off' from politics; we all do. One of my secret vices is, in fact, reading those 18p heavy-duty sexual romantic novelettes. Occasionally I kid myself it's for the purpose of 'research', but the truth is that I need and relish my bit of soft-focus escapism too. Escapism doesn't, unfortunately, make the real world disappear. The fact that the boys have provided us with some updated fantasies – *The Bionic Woman*, *Charlie's Angels*, *Hart to Hart*, *Emmanuelle* – doesn't mean that most of us can now leap the eight-foot fence to our mansions while having triple orgasms *and* still never get a hair out of place. Much less does it mean that we have something so mundane but all-important as real equal pay.

It's younger women who most seem to have bought the present-day concessions to women's liberation as proof of an absolute and permanent victory. *Cosmo*, for example, tell me that those who write in to complain at the magazine's 'unnecessarily campaigning tone' are nearly all readers aged between 18 and 25. Older women, I find, are sensibly wary of calling any premature truce; glad for what has changed, but aware that whatever women have gained, whether in political terms or in personal life, it's had to be fought for, every inch. Once you make a gain, you also have to keep your eyes peeled so that it isn't snatched back again. There's a great deal of sneaky rights-erosion going on at the moment, which is, I suppose, why it's so useful to try to persuade us that the female nirvana has already arrived.

After all, we're now allowed to have outside jobs as well as bear children and run homes – isn't that liberation? Your local nursery may have closed, and hubby may still not know the difference between a lavatory brush and the leeks you're cutting up for his dinner, but if playing superwoman leaves you too tired for your other new role of nighttime sex siren, then that's your problem. If Mrs Thatcher can make it out from under, then all women can …

In other words, liberation is just a state of mind – ours. Plum jobs, multiple orgasms and non-sexist men are all there for the plucking, if only we've the ovaries to take them. There are in fact no material obstacles in women's way, only our own mental blocks …

As the woman trade unionist said, though, 'My consciousness is fine, it's my *pay* that needs raising.' For women, personal and economic liberation are very much bound up. For example, the average woman worker, with her average wage of £50-odd a week, doesn't need self-assertion therapy so much as greenies in the hand; power you can count. On less than £40 take-home, getting out of a bad marriage is difficult, staying single frightening, and even taking your time to look around before settling down can seem a luxury that just means you'll end up on the shelf.

As for experimenting with love and sex, if you've neither class nor career glamour to carry you through confidently, that can still just earn you the damaged-goods label of easy lay. Economic security is, in the end, the factor that really facilitates choice.

Love may be one ingredient of marriage but the cold fact is that for most women, matrimony also seems their best hope of gaining financial security, social status and protection. But because marriage is an entirely private and supposedly voluntary affair, the bonuses may not arrive. One husband is wonderful with the housekeeping, another gives his wife and children next to nothing and there's no law that obliges him to. One husband makes love, another gets a kick out of rape, and that's also perfectly legal. As for protection, most male violence against women occurs in the home; wife-battering constitutes a quarter of all reported crimes. Nonetheless, even having a batterer around the house accords status, as women who are divorced, widowed, single through choice or circumstance, lesbian or celibate, all know. Bachelor is not a term of derision; spinster is.

> '*Love may be one ingredient of marriage but the cold fact is that for most women, matrimony also seems their best hope of gaining financial security.*'

Even if your man is a dedicated pro-feminist who knows all about clitorises, kids and washing up, private revolutions don't provide all the answers. You may, for example, both want to share childcare, but as men usually earn the higher wage, you're still likely to be left holding the baby. Economic realities have a nasty habit of forcing us to play Tarzan and Jane, Janet and John, whether we want to or not.

Yet still the 'liberation now' salesmen keep up the illusion. Any lingering examples of women's oppression are, they tell us, mere hangovers from more primitive times, which a few reforms and the natural process of evolution will soon set right. No need to push, dear, no need to strain at the leash … trust in us. Feminists are rightly wary of that kind of lullaby.

If women are oppressed, it's because someone, somewhere, has a lot to gain by it. Rule number one: know your enemy, don't fight blind. Joe Bloggs with the Rolls and sweat-shop factories does very well out of the women-work-for-pin-money myth; Joe Bloggs' brother, triumphantly leaving the witness stand, does equally well out of the myth that all women long to be raped. Our freedom is directly opposed to theirs – and of course they aren't going to give up anything without a fight.

But, as you say, not all men are like this. Does feminism mean hating all men? For some feminists it does. And overhearing conversations in queues, clinics, launderettes and disco loos, I'm not convinced that ordinary women are all that undilutedly keen on the male sex either. I don't see 'men-hating' as anything to apologise for; nor, really, is it the point. It's only such a useful and powerful accusation because, very neatly, it turns everything on its head. For centuries men have kept us down, yet for making the eminently healthy response of fighting back, we are charged with starting a sex-war.

One way out is to blame everything on The System. But any power system depends on the support of individuals and, in the fight against sexism, it's not noticeably men who are at the forefront of any barricades. Of course, many men are good and lovely, and if yours is, then that's nice for you. But yelling, 'I'm all right Jill, pull up the ladder,' is neither sisterly nor wise. Certainly not all men are mad-dog rapists, but the fact that individual men choose not to exercise the power which society allows them does not mean that that power no longer exists. Many men do feel oppressed by the alienated, macho role, but watch the cocky swaggers on any football terrace, military parade ground or late-night street and you'll see a hell of a lot who don't. I may reel out of *Apocalypse Now* wondering why, why won't men be more like women instead of obedient death machines, but I still don't intend to turn my feminism into a simple campaign to save men from themselves. Saying, 'Please will you stop standing on my head, I'm sure it must be hurting your foot,' isn't really that effective.

Anger, though, is the unforgivable female sin. It's the anti-feminist accusation I most often hear, even from those who now say they accept our ideas and aims, but not our harpY, shrieking ways. Maybe they don't like to be reminded that in the past, speaking in dulcet tones got us nowhere. Both psychology and religion defined obedience and passivity as proof of the normal, well-adjusted female. Calling us mad or bad if we yell: 'Stop! This hurts!' was really quite a clever move.

Feminist culture has, therefore, deliberately 'reclaimed' the insults tradition-ally used against wayward women. Virago books, Deviant records, Monstrous Regiment theatre group, the magazines *Spare Rib*, *Scarlet Woman* and *Shrew* are all, by their very names, giving the boys and their labels a delighted two-fingers.

In the face of opposition, or just indifference, it took anger for feminists to organise the refuges for battered women, the rape crisis centres, the tens of thousands of people demonstrating for abortion rights, and the hundreds of books and pamphlets which have helped popularise feminist ideas. When there's so much still to achieve, and so many gains under attack, it's hardly time to replace our scowls with grateful grins.

Yet, at times, I'm tempted to do just that. Because there's actually something rather comforting about refusing to see. Feminism can hurt, for suddenly there's a vast difference between the world as you want it to be, and the world as it actually is. Raising your consciousness can also mean lowering your threshold to pain. The female casualty lists, when you start to add them up, are frighteningly high. But squeezing your eyes tight shut doesn't make the bogeys go away, or the bricks stop coming. It just means that you're not able to dodge them effec-tively, or to spot the hands ready to help if ever you really do get stuck in the rubble.

> *'I don't see "men-hating" as anything to apologise for; nor, really, is it the point.'*

Not everything in the women's movement is rosy. Some aspects drive me to distraction, and some feminists fill me with less than a gush of sisterly love, especially the minority who act more-feminist-than-thou and parade their lifestyle as the only right one. I don't like to be on the receiving end of that, and I like it even less when women new to the movement tell me that, for turning up wearing a wedding ring instead of an array of badges, a flowery dress instead of plimsolls and dungarees, they've felt ignored or looked down on by 'real' feminists. Sometimes that first experience of being treated as some sort of traitor is all they stay long enough to see.

The real tragedy of such superiority is that it alienates women from feminism. Each woman has to find her own way, her own solutions, and in her own time. Some of us even have to find out the hard way. I, for example, still enjoy wearing my glad rags but do, now, omit the five-inch heels I was once so fond of. You see, the feminist truth about fashion shoes being a modern form of foot-binding came home to me when I hurried to catch a train, and instead of breaking my heel broke my jaw. I wouldn't, however, judge any woman by the fact she wore stilettos instead of Dr Martin boots (though I might, for her own good, saw the heels off while she wasn't looking).

Women's liberation is too important for any one group of women to claim as their preserve, particularly now that we've hit the hard, hard eighties. If feminism isn't to be written off as another impractical dream of the idealistic, boom-time sixties and wilting seventies, we need to be organised and outward-looking, constantly welcoming new women and new ideas. Perhaps, most of all, we need to remember that the movement belongs to all women. ■

You know you're a feminist when ...

October 1993

- You get cross with men who prefer you not to speak your mind.

  - You realise that while motherhood is praised to the skies, real-life mothers get little help from society.

- You wonder why you're constantly interrupted by men at meetings.

  - You don't mind if you are earning more than your boyfriend/husband.

- You wanted to play football at school but felt cheated when you were stopped because you were a girl.

  - You're irritated when you're having a drink with a girlfriend and men assume you want to be picked up.

- You ask yourself why unattractive men over 40 and attractive women under 40 land all the best jobs on television.

  - You drag a pram up yet another steep flight of stairs and realise that the world was designed by men with no children.

- It annoys you to think that women are paid 25 per cent less than men.

- You clean the bathroom for the 51st weekend in a row and your partner doesn't understand why you're so angry.

- You wish people would mind their own business when everyone assumes, rightly or wrongly, that you're going to have children.

- You're fed up with the thought that some day you will have to choose between children and a career.

- If you see one more helpless woman in a film trying (and not succeeding) to escape from a predatory man, you'll *scream*.

- You recognise the ghetto you are in when you look around your office and see most of the typist/ secretarial roles are occupied by women.

- You are accused loudly of being a feminist and agree – wholeheartedly.

- You just cannot comprehend how judges can blame young girls for being raped while letting their older male offenders go free.

- You can't help noticing how women at work are either 'girls' or 'career women' while their male counterparts are never 'boys' or 'career men'.

- You realise it is easier for men to take a day off work for a corporate jolly than it is for women to take a day off to look after a sick child.

- You have discovered the feminist's catch-22: that while trying to point out the unfairness in society (e.g. how single parents need more support), women end up getting blamed for society's ills (i.e. single *mothers* breed delinquent children).

  - You would like to see men's violence being taken more seriously by a society which increasingly curbs women's freedom in the name of safety.

- You are stunned to learn that the penalty for sexual abuse of a male minor is twice that for abuse of a female minor.

  - You're concerned when you hear that single women tend to live longer than married women, whereas married men tend to live longer than single men.

- You lobby your MP on issues to improve life for women and men whenever you can.

  - You cheered loudly when the General Synod voted in favour of the ordination of women parties.

- You understand how a man's gender *allows* him to do things (i.e. walk alone at night, be aggressive) whereas a woman's limits hers.

  - Despite all the inequalities, you're glad that you're a woman. ■

Feminists who strip

If you thought strippers were the epitome of unre-constructed, non-feminist woman, think again. Post Porn Modernists bare all in the name of art and politics.
Melissa Benn
October 1995

The scene: a darkened bar in London's Camden Town. Young and old, men and women, gay and straight rub shoulders in the audience. On stage, dressed in a black cloak and leopard G-string, Marisa Carr, 24, dancer and performance activist extraordinaire, is satirising the great British breakfast. She massages her pubic bone with a string of uncooked sausages and cracks eggs over her naked breasts. But the use of food is not the only thing that is different from a run-of-the-mill strip show. As she works, Marisa sings politi-cised, ironic versions of songs, like 'Oom-pa-pa' from the stage show *Oliver!* And music-hall classics like 'Don't Put Your Daughter on the Stage, Mrs Worthington'.

Next on is Miss Daisy (alias Alison Cocks), aged 27. Bearing a close resemblance to Margi Clarke, she, too, wears a black cloak, though, this time, accessorised with a pointed witch's hat. She strips down to her knee-high black lace-up boots, but this is no ordinary 'sex act'. In between bottom-juts and breast fondling, Miss Daisy offers up her frank opinions on the Criminal Justice Act and 'rich Tory bastards'.

The audience is dazed … and amused. A bunch of young, punky women, sitting round a table at the back of the room, whoop with delight at the performers. They understand exactly what's going on. It's the odd 'straight' punter who has wandered in off the street who seems shocked at this subversion of his usual Saturday afternoon entertainment.

Perhaps this specimen of Ordinary Bloke can be forgiven for missing the point. As if in a dream, he has stumbled upon a new kind of performance which, though it looks familiar, conforms to none of the expected rules of public sex. For this is the place where performance art meets the traditional sex show, where punk feminism meets the larger-than-life gestures of the Edwardian music-hall.

Welcome to Post Porn Modernism, a form of politicised pornography so christened by American performance artist Annie Sprinkle. It was Annie and fellow performance artist Jennifer Blowdryer who, in the mid-eighties, conceived the idea of a subversive, politicised sex/art cabaret act and first put on a show in a New York burlesque strip joint. Now, after nearly ten years of performing across the States, mainly in underground, gay and fetish clubs, the idea has made it to the mainstream circuit in puritan old Britain.

Marisa, Miss Daisy and their colleague, Tutu, are just three of Post Porn Modernism's British exponents. For such young women – at 28, Tutu is the eldest – they have a clutch of impressive CVs: Marisa has worked with Annie Sprinkle, and has performed in New York, Amsterdam, Paris, Glasgow and at London's ICA; Miss Daisy has worked in a variety of European peep-shows; Tutu is an impressario who stages club nights at London venues like Heaven and The Fridge.

They are also highly qualified. Marisa has a first-class honours degree in Visual and Performance Art from Brighton University and, before that, studied dance at the Laban Centre at London's Goldsmith's College. Among her influences, she cites the punk and feminist movements and a generation of rebel women artists, including musician Patti Smith and writer Kathy Acker. She is particularly interested in 'traditional forms of women's entertainment, be it belly-dancing, the vaudeville show or the music-hall. And playing with the idea of woman as witch, murderess, eccentric and neurotic.' It is, she says, 'precisely because women have been defined by their sexuality in Western culture that sexual performance is the very place where we can subvert traditional ideas most successfully.'

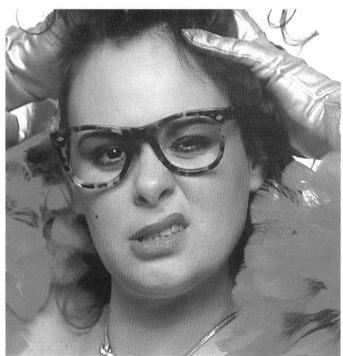

Miss Daisy is studying for a combined degree in Women's Studies and Theatre Studies at the University of North London. She says, 'I love theatre but I'm sad there are so many sexual taboos in theatre work. Equally, I love stripping, but I'm sad that it's so dominated by the male gaze.' Like Marisa, the image of the witch figures prominently in Miss Daisy's work. In her first TV appearance – a short, gloriously dirty strip to be shown in Channel 4's new access slot, *Takeover TV*, in May – the voice-over is a sombre reminder of the horrendous treatment handed out to so-called witches in medieval England. It doesn't take much imagination to see the parallels between the opprobrium that such women incurred 500 years ago and the full weight of disapproval heaped upon the likes of Marisa, Miss Daisy and Tutu.

For, make no mistake, this trio's stuff is disconcertingly sexy, breaching the accepted view that to be turned on is a private matter between the desiring viewer and the compliant performer. The Post Porn Modernists bring it all out into the open. And, as they work, every word, movement and look is saying, 'I'm doing this for myself as much as for you.'

So is this what distinguishes them from ordinary strippers? While all three are keen to point out their respect for more conventional sex workers, they are quite clear in their answer: it's the context and the control that make the difference.

Miss Daisy started off by doing traditional stripping to finance her way through college: 'I was working in a big venue in Portugal and I just couldn't do it – the passive, "come hither" stuff – so I decided to take control of my performance. I put on Doc Martens and had David Bowie's *Rebel, Rebel* as a soundtrack, and I was just much more aggressive, talking to the audience. I loved it. And they loved it.'

Marisa and Miss Daisy often talk out loud during their shows. As Miss Daisy says, 'It changes the whole thing, because you're not an object any more. You're a subject. And when I talk, I really get off on what I'm saying and on my own fantasies, on confronting the audience with nudity.' And then there are the jokes – 'the ironic little references,' as Marisa puts it, 'that make it different from a Soho strip bar. Humour is essential. Humour communicates wisdom.'

For Tutu, power is the key: 'To me as a kid, a call-girl or stripper was a powerful, glamorous figure,' she says. 'She made her own money. She got dressed up in the best clothes, the highest heels, the best make-up. That's what I like to do. I love standing up in front of people and everybody going, 'Yeah, that gets my rocks off!' It doesn't make me feel degraded. Why should being beautiful be degrading?'

They are all committed feminists, for whom feminism means the rights of women to control and explore their own sexuality without guilt. All three support Feminists Against Censorship, a group campaigning for fewer controls on sexual material and greater erotic freedom for women.

Marisa says, 'Much of the feminism of the last three decades that was critical of pornography and of male violence to women was very important to us. But the agenda has changed now. Sex and sexual expression can be very positive for women.'

Not surprisingly, their work does arouse hostility and confusion among women of a different era or with other politics. 'Sometimes, with an all-female audience, you can see they don't know quite how to react,' says Tutu. 'They're looking at the woman next to them to see what she's thinking. If she's laughing or cheering, then that's OK. Then they'll feel free to join in.'

They've had their share of barracking, too. Tutu recalls, 'I was handing out leaflets for a show and a woman started shouting at me, 'Tits and ass, tits and ass – that's all it ever is. Why do you have to degrade yourself? Aren't you worth more than that?' Of course I am. My sexuality is only part of what I do. But it's a valuable part.'

Funnily enough, it's now men that they count as their most difficult audience – but for all the right reasons. Tutu says, 'Whereas older men still see women's sexuality as something they own, young men want to see women being sexy, but they don't want to feel they're degrading their girlfriends. They've grown up in a culture where women are equal, get equal jobs. So they're confused.' Miss Daisy agrees: 'Younger men really want to know we're having a good time – "Are you enjoying it? Oh, all right, if you are, then we can."'

Enjoyment is at the heart of the work of the Post Porn Modernists. But it has its serious edge. Ironically, watching Miss Daisy, Marisa and Tutu in performance made me think more about womanhood than sex: about what constitutes shame. And nakedness. About the terrible restraint that 'modesty' and 'femininity' can represent. And it made me glad that a group of young women has got the guts – and the art – to go out naked into the world and challenge all that conformist nonsense. In so doing, they're remaking sexual politics for the millennium and reviving what was always the best element of feminism – women's liberation. ■

CHAPTER 4

OH, THE AGONY OF IT ...

The agony pages of a magazine are a curious phenomenon. Readers' letters cannot be answered personally – you'd need an entire team to deal with the flood of mail – and the writer of a letter will probably never see her problem addressed in the magazine. The time lag between writing and the first chance of it appearing on the page is about three months, and if *Cosmopolitan*'s Irma Kurtz receives a monthly postbag of 300 letters, not more than about four or five of these will end up in print. The writer of the letter is quite aware of this, so why on earth does she bother?

The reader's concerns are most certainly genuine. By the time she writes a letter you can be sure that her problem has been with her for some time. She *needs* to express what's on her mind. The mere act of writing it down provides relief, or as Irma says, 'It can be a helpful and calming process to put words on paper.' Posting – or e-mailing a letter – is the second step towards some kind of resolution. 'Often,' says Irma, 'the writer ends her letter by saying something like: "even if you don't answer this, it has helped to write it down." Now, perhaps, she can move on and decide what to do for herself.'

Agony columns were a staple of women's magazines long before the birth of *Cosmopolitan*, and they are as popular today as ever. The reason for their popularity is simple – if the specifics are personal to the writer, the themes – jealousy, fidelity, self-esteem – are universal. Up to a point, everyone can identify.

Irma describes it this way: 'The advice offered has to contain something that will be valid for more than the individual: some general truth, or some attitude that starts the readers thinking for themselves, whether in agreement or disagreement. It is probably the one job where age helps. Wisdom is the mature product of common sense: it takes time and experience to develop. They come to us for wisdom, just as women used to go to the white witch at the bottom of the lane for advice and love potions. I think it is possible to see us as a refuge from fashion: something grounded.'

But the agony column isn't just about advice, it's also entertainment. You could call it entertainment at the expense of other people's misery, but that would be to miss the point. All of us are endlessly curious about the way people live their everyday lives and deal with their everyday dilemmas. And in the hands of Irma Kurtz – at 26 years, *Cosmopolitan*'s most enduring contributor – the agony column is a gripping read. Irma pulls no punches. She purveys her wisdom in the form of pithy journalism and tough love. She has no truck with badly behaved men – or the women who put up with them. She gives the reader courage and she even cracks a few jokes.

Irma's agony years

Writing in *Cosmopolitan's* 30th anniversary issue, **Irma Kurtz** looked back on 26 years of advice to reveal how sexual and emotional problems have changed through the decades.

The Agony Column began for me a long time ago when I was a teenager, waiting on a subway platform in Manhattan. 'Excuse me,' said a voice behind me. I turned and saw a woman more than twice my age in tears. 'My husband has left me and the kids for his twenty-year-old hairdresser. What am I going to do?' Without so much as asking the first question I would ask now ('Is his hairdresser a man or a woman?') I sized her up and told her: 'First, get angry. Then, get a lawyer. After that, get a life, a good life. Try not to say anything bad about him to the kids, they'll find out on their own what a jerk he is.'

You see, agony aunts are born, not made. An agony aunt is the stranger waiting for a train or bus that you find yourself confiding in. Why? Because she is endlessly nosy about other people and you sense that she will listen with interest. And because she is very bossy, she will answer honestly, tell you what she thinks or has learned through experience and observation, not what she has been taught by others to think, and never what she thinks she should think. In 1976, one of the early editors of *Cosmo* had the intuition to see that in me – already a contributor of a few years' standing – she had a born agony aunt.

'You're so bossy. You're so nosy,' she said. 'Will you write an advice column for us?'

'I cannot think of anything I'd rather do,' I replied, 'but only if you promise not to call it an advice column, it has to be "The Agony Column".'

So, have the problems changed in all the years since that fateful day? You bet. But in a way, they haven't changed at all. The great underlying problem has been with us – women – since the first female saw herself reflected in a pond and thought she was too fat or flat or busty for any man to want to drag her back to his cave. From her false self-image and subsequent lack of confidence grew the major ills of womankind, among them, the agony of habitual jealousy that arose in the very first 'Agony Column' and continues to pop up regularly.

For example, 'Every time my boyfriend phones to say he is working late, I'm compelled to ring back and check on him. At parties, I am glued to his side. Do I love him too much?'

And the reply in 1976 was as it would be now: 'Jealousy is never a sign of love; it is always in proportion to insecurity. Unless this man is deliberately behaving in a way to arouse jealousy in you because he enjoys it as a power trip, your possessiveness springs from a secret fear within yourself that you do not deserve to be loved. Find the fear and face it, then put an end to it.'

One woman is in love with her boss, another with her best friend's boyfriend, while a third loves nobody and hates sex; lonely singles looking for men; partners, betrayed and forgiving, who wonder when their trust will return: these problems and others, like unbounded sexual jealousy, were with us in the seventies, eighties and nineties and probably the preceding decades, too, and they're with us now.

However, those early days saw new problems; problems of decision-making that were very much of the era, emerging straight out of our recent liberation and equalisation in status.

'At 26, with a successful career, I married a good-looking architect,' wrote one *Cosmo* reader in the seventies. 'We go to parties and holiday in France. He likes the free life and hates the idea of a sensible family car. But I long to have babies and be a cabbage…'

'Whatever put the idea into your head,' I asked back, 'that bringing up children and tending a house were passive or mindless? Are you sure you're not already a cabbage who thinks it would be nice to be a ratatouille…?

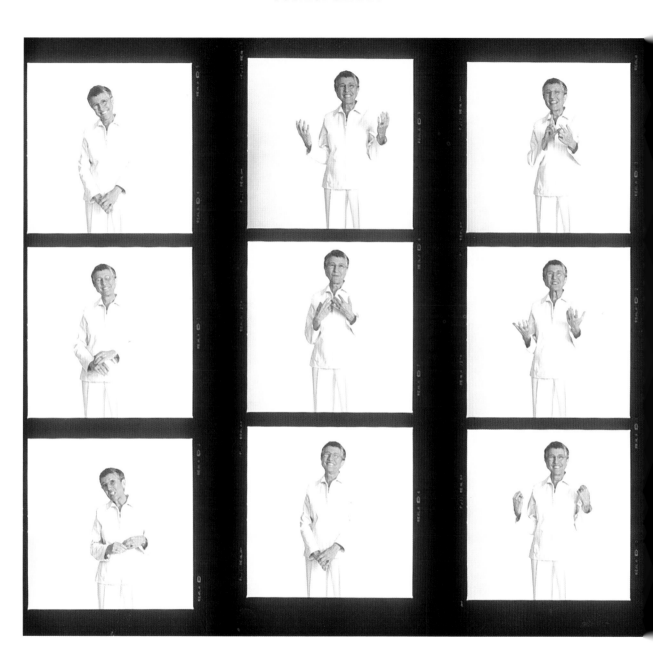

Irma Kurtz, for 26 years **Cosmopolitan**'s agony aunt.

From my vantage point now, I can see that what gave her the idea was a real prejudice, in the newly liberated seventies, against women who did not choose to avail themselves of new opportunities: women who chose not to – as if choosing not to wasn't choosing, too.

In fact, choices brought plenty of new agony in the seventies. One reader wrote: 'I am 26 and have a flat and a good job. My boyfriend's being transferred out of London for two years. He says if I loved him, I would follow…'. Her reluctance was not new, many women have hated leaving their childhood home and family, even for love. But to hate to leave her own flat and good job – that was new agony back when *Cosmo* was starting out.

There were fewer and fewer of such either/or problems in the eighties and hardly any arrive now from energetic *Cosmo* readers who expect to have it all (although maybe not all at the same time) with ideal partners who want to share it all. These days, I might wonder in print why he does not feel compelled to *stay* for *her* sake? Although in the end I would probably say exactly what I said then: 'Give it a few months, see how you fare as a couple temporarily apart and let the decision make itself.'

The vastly increased speed of modern travel and communications lightened the agony of lovers' separation in the nineties and the naughty noughties. Interestingly, as more and more agony arrives by email instead of old-fashioned snail-mail, modern problems are set out in a more concise manner. On the other hand, the price of modern speed and brevity is handwriting, colour of ink, underlining and scratching out, and other clues beyond words to the personality of the writer.

Of the many changes in the nature of agony over the years, none is greater than the relationship between a woman and her parents. In virtually every other issue of early 'Agony Columns' was a letter from someone, often well into her twenties, worried about parental disapproval. It is as if we all lived in some other country back then for, with rare exceptions nowadays, it is only young people raised in more strict cultures than ours who communicate agonising fear of parental disapproval.

The conflicts were not just about relationships, they often concerned career choices and style of life. 'I am twenty, I want to live in a flat with two friends, but I am afraid to tell my parents…' (1976). 'My husband has been unfaithful almost since our wedding. I want to leave him, but my mum thinks he is wonderful…' (1978). 'I am 27. I feel miserable and in a rut. How can I tell my parents who are very proud of my progress at work that I want to go and live abroad?' (1980).

Towards the end of the seventies, when womankind was supposedly released into uninhibited, rampaging sex, there were still alarming lapses of knowledge. 'My boyfriend tells me he is a masochist. What am I to expect?' wrote one reader. 'A lot of hard work,' I told her, 'for a few laughs.'

In the po-faced eighties and perhaps even now, I would have felt required to explain exactly what masochism was, how some people of both sexes get that way, and how there are never enough sadists to go around. But it is my impression people felt freer to joke more about sex and found it funnier, if not more fun, in the pre-AIDS decades.

'I have heard it is harmful to have sex when you're not fully physically developed,' wrote a reader back in 1978. 'When I was fourteen, I had intercourse twice but no more in the four years since. Has this caused me any harm? Will my breasts remain small? Will I ever grow into a woman or will I remain the same until I start to age? Do I have to wait until I am 21 before I have sex again? I am so worried I might never have the body of a normal woman.'

Whatever objections people have to this day about sex education for the young, every current *Cosmo* reader knows that 'harmful' includes emotional and psychological damage. Sex, we now know and teach young people, has a more resonant effect on us than the sheer physicality that this under-educated child of the seventies ascribed to it.

Mind you, some pretty naïve letters arrived even into the super-sophisticated recent decades. How about this one from the mid-eighties? 'My boyfriend wants to try the "69" position. Am I going out with a pervert?' Here we are, only a few years later in the greater scheme of things, and the expression '69' is out of fashion; 'oral sex' or fellatio and cunnilingus (a tongue-twister if ever there was one!), sound nicer to the modern ear. 'Is he a pervert?' I replied then, as still holds true today about many sexual matters: 'On the contrary! Congratulations! Most of the letters I receive from women make the opposite complaint! Not why does he want it? But why won't he do it?'

Irma – The Facts

• Irma, 66, has contributed to *Cosmo* since its launch. Her first Agony Column started 26 years ago in May 1976.

• She receives 300 letters a month in the UK asking for advice.

• Irma is the agony aunt for US *Cosmo* as well, where she receives 2,000 letters a month.

• 90 per cent of the letters are about relationships, half of those are about sex.

• The most common question is, 'Why won't he do what I want him to do?'

• The few letters she receives from men are from those who dress in women's clothes.

As soon as the Pill came on the scene many years ago, we started going on and on about it as if there were only one available. Nowadays there are lots more pills around, good and bad, than we ever dreamed of in the pre-Prozac era when *Cosmo* was in its infancy.

'I am worried about my boyfriend. He is a man of 55 (I am twenty) and he is unable to fulfil me sexually. He begins to cry when he tries to reach a climax. I comfort him… but he says he is too old.' No doubt I would lecture her now just as I did then about the peculiarity of calling a man of 55 her 'boyfriend'. But I could soften my ticking-off with a recommendation to ask his doctor about Viagra, a drug that was just a gleam in grandad's eye back in the seventies when this letter was written.

In fact, more than any psychological changes since then, and as much as social changes, medical science has radically altered and added to the advice business. To look back at women who wrote to *Cosmo* in the early days because they were troubled by issues of fertility, PMS and, in one case, a threatened masectomy makes me sad. There was little to offer but sympathy.

Wonderful and astounding advances have been made in these areas since *Cosmo* was born 30 years ago. However, recently I have found myself worried by the falling-off of questions dealing with sexually transmitted infections – they used to come by the sackful in the paranoid eighties. We can treat most of them now, yes, and cure many. And the condom, hardly credited except as a fall-back contraceptive until the mid-eighties, has become essential. But STIs have not gone away. We have a responsibility never to forget about them as a serious risk of all sexual contacts.

Equally, we women must not grow complacent about our hard-won right to abortion, no matter how sorrowfully undertaken, when we know it is the only recourse.

Of all the agony that has come my way there is one eternally asked question that I hope (hopelessly) never ever to hear again. 'He doesn't like my friends/he can't get it up/he never says he loves me,' write the modern girl as her fore-mothers before her.

'Sort him out,' I tell her, 'ease him into it, teach him to know better. Or find somebody who does what your current partner won't or cannot do.' Then I read on, and too often the woman of this new century echoes the female line before: 'What's wrong with me?' '*Nothing* is wrong with you,' I want to scream. 'Nothing! Tell *him* to drop me a line. You are the greatest, the best. Just like *Cosmo*, you are better than ever!'. ∎

For almost a decade – starting in the mid-eighties, psychologist Tom Crabtree wrote the column 'On The Couch'. Lying back on his Le Corbusier chaise longue, balding, bow-tied, with a bushy moustache and a broad grin, middle-aged Tom made an unlikely pin-up. But the readers adored him. Quite a few of them wanted to marry him (Tom was already married). We decided to invite some of his fans along to meet him one lunchtime so he could hear at first hand the interests and concerns of *Cosmo* readers … and put a small notice in the magazine outlining the details. An astonishing 600 readers requested the pleasure of his company.

Tom's speciality was siding with the reader against all the rotten men they encountered. He gave them hope – that out there there were good men, caring men, romantic men, men who understood, men who weren't macho, men who'd stay true, men, in fact, who were just like Tom. Sadly there isn't enough of him to go round.

On the couch with Tom Crabtree

'Hate does *you* more harm than
the person you hate'
November 1987

Q How can I stop hating someone? A man let me down when I was at the weakest and most vulnerable point in my life. Now I'm struggling to get back to normality and my hatred of this person is blocking the way to me being healed. I can't control my feelings and thoughts. I've tried pitying him and praying for him – both of which have helped for a short while – but this destructive emotion seems to be taking over and I think of little else on and off all day. Please help. X.

A Dear X. The first thing is not to feel too guilty about it. Don't let your super-ego point the fickle finger of fault at you. *Hate if you want to*. Everyone does at some time or other. I used to hate my brother; I used to pray to God to send me a machine gun so that justice could be done. Then I learned that hate demeans you; it does *you* a great deal more harm than the person you hate.

Hate is distilled animosity; it's a poison within the soul. With hate, we project the nastiest bits of ourselves on to someone else; we hate the most those we have loved the best and who didn't respect that love or made us feel bad.

Hate is a consuming passion. It takes up your whole being, uses up your energy, cuts off your potential for love, friendship and happiness. It isolates and demeans you. What is the effect of all this on the person you hate? Nothing. You're the one who suffers.

Hate – like guilt or jealousy – is a useless, destructive emotion. It is a per-version, caused by pride. Some people hate for a lifetime; they lose the ability to love. So why do we do it? If we choose to hate, it is because it saves us the trouble of doing something positive about ourselves and our situation.

Consider what you *could* do. You could write your man a letter and tell him exactly what you think of his behaviour, his treatment of you. Or you could phone him up and do the same. This will take courage but you're entitled to do it. Concentrate on his behaviour. Don't call him a rat. Just say his behaviour was appalling (if it was). It's your right.

This man has pierced your heart, exposed your feelings of inadequacy and vulnerability. Now is the time to regain your self-respect. You can do that *not* by praying for him but by telling him what you think about what he did to you, and how hurt you were. Tell him the score. Do what is fair, right and positive (and maintain your self-respect). Don't sit in your room, all by yourself, hating. Give that nasty blighter a bit of verbal stick – then shun him, let him go. We're fools to waste time on people who bring out the worst in us.

Here's a Six Point Plan to help win back your self-respect:

Talk to someone about your feelings. If you're feeling desperate, ring the Samaritans (their number's in the local phone book). They'll understand. Find a friend and describe your feelings, your fear of the awesome power of the hatred within you. It does help to talk about our feelings; it's always worse to keep negative emotions locked up inside us.

Don't condemn yourself. He's the one who lacks humanity, not you. You acted well; he behaved badly. Why be so hard on yourself? Start eating properly again, getting some sleep, looking after yourself. Make some new friends, get out and start to live again. Get out of that theatre of hate. That horrible play's over. Why punish yourself when you've done nothing?

Make a list of the things he did that you thought were wrong or that hurt you. Examine that list; make sure it's fair and accurate. Send it to him to let him know how he let you down. Why keep it all to yourself? That makes hate grow, not die.

Limit your hate. I can't order you to give up your hate of this man. If you must hate, hate for five minutes each day. Think of him and say, 'I really hate you.' If you hate all of the time it's heaping on the self-punishment. Why do it?

Ask yourself, 'Is he really worth it?' Be honest (and show courage). Is this man worth thinking/worrying about? (Never mind hating.) What has he done for you? What are his feelings towards you? Does he respect you, care about you, make you feel good? If all he has done is to bring you pain, confusion, feelings of inadequacy, then let him go and play his little games elsewhere. Good riddance.

Say to yourself, 'I'm worth better'. You are. Why waste time on this sort of horrible creature? Why demean yourself by stooping to dislike him, or resorting to hate? Let the blighter go; tell him what you think (so he is less inclined to treat others in the same way) and say, 'That's me out of it'. He's not worth a hair on your head, not worth a line in your life-script. Don't make a tragedy of your life with a rat occupying centre stage. ■

Tom's gentle philosophical approach made you want to hug him and take him home with you to meet your mum (she'd probably want to keep him for herself). Despite his dark good looks and trendy suit, readers might not feel quite so gooey about Dr Raj Persaud, *Cosmopolitan*'s resident shrink, first introduced to the reader in 1997. 'The Session' with Dr Persaud, in which he explores one reader's problem, in a one-to-one dialogue, is not remotely touchy-feely, nor would you expect it to be, given that Dr Persaud is a highly respected consultant psychiatrist at The Maudsley Hospital. Although casually cross-legged in his photo, posed to look as though he's conversing with someone just beyond the frame of the picture, the mood conveyed is still one of detached professionalism. By comparison, the world according to Tom Crabtree seems positively quaint.

The Session with Dr Raj Persaud

DEAR DR PERSAUD, I'm getting into a lot of conflict with everyone around me about my weight. My boyfriend, family and friends keep going on at me that I am too thin and should put on weight, but I feel fine as I am. Why can't they just leave me alone? Please help, Martha, 20 January 2002

DR RAJ PERSAUD What do you weigh and how tall are you?
MARTHA Oh God, you aren't going to start by going on about those dreadful weight charts are you? I'm a very small-framed person so I'm not convinced they apply to me at all.

DR Let's cross the bridge about how relevant the charts are to you after we have taken a look at what you actually weigh. Knowing the actual numbers is a good basis for a discussion rather than just how you look or how you feel – which can be subjective – and might change according to your mood.

MARTHA Well I'm 5ft 1in and the last time I weighed myself I was 6^{1}_{2} st.

DR Well, according to my charts you are at least a stone under the biologically healthy minimum weight for a woman of your height. Has no one ever told you that before?

MARTHA Not so directly – I have been to the doctor at the request of my parents and she just said I was a bit on the thin side. But I feel fine.

DR Well when your weight gets too low, your body stops working properly in terms of its biological functions – for example your periods can become inter-mittent or stop altogether – which is a sure sign that something isn't working inside your body because your weight has dropped too much.

MARTHA Sure, I had a brief episode a year ago when my periods lost their regularity, but that hasn't happened since. Isn't it possible I'm just naturally thin? Surely not everyone off the scale on those charts is inevitably abnormal?

DR That's a good point – there is something called the 'Slimderella Complex' of a group of women who do appear to be naturally thin and no matter how hard they genuinely try they can't seem to gain weight. But the key point and possible difference between them and you is that they *feel* too thin and want to gain weight. But your situation may be different – are you happy being so thin? It doesn't appear as if you want to gain weight?

'The tight control you believe you have over your weight means you have lost control everywhere else.'

MARTHA No I don't want to gain at all, if anything I'm sure I am still a little overweight for my frame. I feel fat around my thighs and hips and I think if I could lose a little there, I would feel happier with my body. It's because I'm not happy with my body that I get upset with everyone going on at me about it and drawing attention to it – it makes me feel more self-conscious and I think it's counterproductive. When I get upset I just stop eating altogether.

DR Do you recall a time when you felt you were your perfect weight – how did you feel then about things in general?

MARTHA Yes, about a year ago I was very close and that was when I was a bit thinner than I am now. I suppose I hark back to then a lot and dream of get-ting back to that weight.

DR So do you want to lose more weight really and you are trying to achieve that – how I wonder?

MARTHA I'm not trying that hard because everyone around me keeps watching me like a hawk when I eat, which is in itself really off-putting. I try to skip breakfast and lunch and only eat supper. I go swimming a lot – I competed for my school at national level last year and I am still in training for other competitions coming up.

DR I suspect you weigh yourself a lot as well?

MARTHA At least once a day.

DR I wonder if it's possible that all the unhappiness you attribute to those around you going on about your figure could be down to the excessive preoccupation you have yourself with weight. It might be you are indulging in the classic 'black and white' thinking of those with eating disorders – they assume that everything in the world will be perfect if only they could achieve their ideal weight. Is it not possible to achieve happiness at the weight you are currently at or a bit higher?

MARTHA I don't think so.

DR Why don't we find out what your natural weight is by you eating more naturally – you can carry on with the exercise, but what about three small meals a day – which is more natural than what you are doing at the moment. After all, you don't really think you could spend the rest of your life on one meal a day do you?

MARTHA Now you're beginning to sound like everyone else around me.

DR If everyone around you who cares for you is saying the same, maybe it's time to listen.

MARTHA I suppose deep down I know something is wrong – it's just so terrifying to give up control of my body or my weight. Control is so important to me.

DR I know, but oddly enough the tight control you believe you have over your weight means you have lost control everywhere else. Why not give up a bit of control there to regain control elsewhere, particularly in your relationships which are suffering because of your preoccupation with your weight?

MARTHA I suppose I never thought of the benefits of relaxing a bit on the weight front – I only ever saw the dangers – particularly in terms of becoming fat. I suppose you think I should go back to the GP and get a referral to a dietician and a counsellor for more advice?

DR Absolutely and do some reading – there are some excellent self-help books available on how to conquer an eating disorder.

DR PERSAUD'S COMMENT Martha needs more professional help – a dietician and counsellor – as she has become overly preoccupied with her weight. Although she has set herself a thinness goal she feels will mean happiness when she achieves it, the reality is the process can only result in misery. To get a better idea of her natural weight, she should ask her GP to check her BMI (Body Mass Index) but also take a peek at the family photo album to see what shape her ancestors, who have given her their genes, look like. The best way to gain a healthy body is with plenty of social exercise, and three meals a day. Maintaining fitness should be part of a fun and healthy natural lifestyle, rather than a chore. ■

Dr Linda Papadopolous is a recent addition to the *Cosmopolitan* team. A senior lecturer and course director in counselling psychology at London Guildhall University, she was introduced to *Cosmo* after appearing on *Big Brother*. 'Think of her as your super-qualified best friend,' said the magazine in May 2001, 'who can empathise with your problems, yet can bring her years of training, knowledge and professional expertise into play when offering possible solutions.' As *Cosmo*'s new life and love advisor, the glamorous Dr Linda states, 'As a 29-year-old professional, I *am* a *Cosmo* girl. My psychology training gives me a unique insight into twenty-something women's lives, which is what I want to bring to the magazine.' She goes on to say: 'Everyone has some self-doubt. "Do I look right? Am I in the right job? Will I find the right man?" I don't provide do-it-or-else answers. It's more about finding a way to let answers surface, through humour, gentle probing – or sharing a few glasses of Chardonnay. My column in *Cosmo* will be about just that: friends, relationships and exploring inner desires.'

Dr Linda's 'I'm listening' column takes the form of a dilemma posed by a group of friends who, alongside Dr Linda, chip in with ideas of their own. Like a girl's night in, with Dr Linda as the special guest, it's girly, matey, jolly, jokey ... and hopefully helpful, too. You, the reader, are the eavesdropper – it's the printed version of Reality TV.

So here we have *Cosmo*, 30 years since its launch, in the age of the 'fun, fearless female', running not one, not two, but *three* regular versions of the agony column. We have Irma Kurtz, the revered wise woman, Dr Raj Persaud, the media-friendly shrink, and Dr Linda who, despite her PhD, presents herself as very much one of the girls. Fortunately for the professional advisor, everyday anxieties and major crises, the stuff of real life, are not subject to what's in and what's out; what's fashionable and what's so-last-year. The *Cosmo* reader may like to present herself as 'fun and fearless' and there may be days – or, if she's lucky, whole weeks may go by – when she feels just that. But levels of confidence, self-esteem and self-worth shift like the sands, according to what's going on in our lives. Ecstasy there may be, especially in *Cosmo*'s sexiest confessional stories, but it wouldn't be real life without the agony in between.

Dr Linda's listening:
'How do I find out where I stand?'

You've consummated your relationship and you think your romance has potential. But how do you establish the boundaries without seeming needy? **Dr Linda Papadopoulos** has the answer…

2001

The friends

- *Melissa* Age: 26

Status: dating

Job: fashion journalist

- *Rita* Age: 28

Status: stuck in a bit of a rut

Job: housewife and mother of two

- *Rosy* Age: 26

Status: don't even go there!

Job: estate agent

- *Sarah* Age: got stuck on 29 three years ago

Status: uncertain

Job: something big in the City

I've often tried to explain to my husband – on the rare occasion when he risks saying something like, 'But don't you already have 30 pairs of black shoes?' – that a woman's relationship with footwear is more complex than most men think. There's something about the whole experience of finding, trying on, and finally purchasing those cute kitten heels that's akin to England scoring that winning goal at some big footbally-type competition. He usually just nods and smiles and then tells me how great my latest purchase looks … God I love him!

So when Rosy called on Thursday to ask if I wanted to meet her for a day of expensive shoe shopping I couldn't refuse.

When I get to the first shoe shop to meet Rosy, I find another friend, Antonio, trying to convince her that the £150 red and white checked denim slingbacks in her hand are actually a really good investment – but only if she can manage to walk in them without looking constipated.

Meanwhile Mel and Rita are laughing at Sarah who's become quite aggressive with the (now very frightened) young shop assistant, Fred, who's kneeling at her feet. Sarah's insisting she's never taken a size eight in her life and that the sizing on the designer trainers is clearly wrong. So Fred tries to help her cram the remaining portion of her heel into various dainty pairs.

> *'I've been seeing him for three weeks, but I'm not sure if he's still seeing other people.'*

'Linda, what do you think?' asks Rosy as she limps up and down in front of the mirror.

'They're cool if you plan on sitting down all night – or want to walk like a pregnant duck!' shouts Mel across the vast display of stilettos to die for.

'I'm serious,' says Rosy, looking at me in desperation. 'I'm meeting Jasper again this week, it all seems to be going so well, and I want to look perfect.'

'The girl's loved up!' coos Antonio, while trying to get Fred's attention with exaggerated gestures.

'Well I'm not sure,' replies Rosy.

'Why not honey?' asks Antonio, who's now bending over in front of Fred to pick up a shoe horn he didn't need.

'It's just that I haven't quite figured out if we're "exclusive" yet,' says Rosy looking puzzled. 'I've been seeing him for three weeks now and I really like him, but I'm not sure if he's still seeing other people and expecting me to do the same.'

At this point the rest of the girls come over to join us, most of them wearing mismatched shoes – and Sarah's now crammed her foot into patent leather stilettos with titanium heels which look more like lethal weapons than footwear.

'Why don't you just ask him?' asks Rita.

'She can't do that!' snaps Mel. 'She'll come across all needy.'

'Well, my mother says, keep your options open: "Date as many men as you like, until he's put a rock on your finger,"' giggles Rita, flashing her emerald-cut diamond.

'I don't know,' argues Sarah. 'I've always thought that once you've exchanged bodily fluids, the relationship becomes exclusive.'

'What!? You're exclusive as soon as you kiss? Now that would make life difficult!,' says Antonio, who still has one eye on Fred.

'Come on Linda,' says Rita hopefully. 'Take off those heels and tell us what you think Rosy should do.'

'Well, there is no hard and fast rule for this one, since different cultures and generations have different views on dating. So focus on what feels right for you. As it stands, it sounds as if you think you've entered that stage of a relationship where you need to redefine the boundaries, or maybe even set up some new ones,' I say.

'Yes, but only if he wants to. I'm just not sure what to do,' says Rosy. 'Maybe you're unsure about what to do because you're not clear about how he feels, so you're afraid of rejection,' I suggest.

'That and looking stupid,' adds Rosy, stood on one leg in her purple tracksuit bottoms and check-patterned stilettos.

'So there's also something about being afraid that the balance of power between you will be affected if you ask first,' I add.

'Well, yes. I would give him the upper hand,' says Rosy worriedly.

'Honey you so don't want to be a whiny woman who pressures her man into commitment!' says Sarah, adopting the persona of her cyber weapon-like shoes.

I step in to save Rosy from the not-very-constructive comments. 'That's another thing. You're afraid that by clarifying this, you'll take the "dependent girlfriend" role.'

Psychologist Dr Linda Papadopoulus.

'But I suppose I am. So what do I do?'

'Well first, be clear about why you're asking what you're asking. Explain that you don't want to put pressure on the relationship, but you do want to be clear about the boundaries, so that you have a better chance of surviving as a couple.

Then try to pitch the discussion at a more rational – rather than emotional – level. This will make you feel more confident and send the message that you aren't dependent, but that you simply know what you want.'

'OK, so you mean talk like equals about what's best for the relationship, and not just for me?' asks Rosy.

'Yes – almost like a business contract where you negotiate common goals. And finally, don't set it up as an 'either/or' question, but as an open and ongoing discussion where you can both explore the pros and cons of the relationship.'

'Cool, I'll try it,' says Rosy.

'Don't worry sweetie,' giggles Antonio. 'Failing that, you can always threaten him with Sarah's titanium shoe weapons!' ◼

CHAPTER 5

JOBS FOR THE GIRLS

If sex was the topic that the made the news, got *Cosmo* talked about and moved copies – fast – off the newsagents shelves, it was in the arena of the workplace that *Cosmo* had equal, and from the late seventies to mid-nineties possibly more, impact on women's lives.

When *Cosmo* launched in 1972, the best advice it could think up for young women in search of rewarding work, was to find a job 'where the men are'. A story on the glamorous world of advertising, for example, profiled four good-looking – and available – young bachelors who earned loads of dosh. A story on getting a job in finance followed the same format. We didn't tell the reader *how* to get a job in advertising or the money markets, or indeed exactly what kind of work she might *do* in advertising or the city. The underlying assumption was that once you were in – as a receptionist or secretary – the rest would follow. No, not recognition, and no, not promotion, but dates, hot dates, with the sexy power brokers.

We wised up quickly. Penny Vincenzi (the same Penny who went on to become a best-selling novelist) alerted readers to the idea of a career in retailing. Penny remembered the warnings about shop girls that she'd received at school. 'If you don't start doing a bit better than this,' her form mistress had informed the class 'you'll end up working in a shop.' 'This pronouncement,' wrote Penny, 'was supposed to send shivers of dread down our girlish spines, synonymous, it seemed, with "Going on the Streets".'

'We might have done well to have gone to the said shops and started working there,' Penny continued. ' If we'd been clever, resourceful and fairly determined, we could have progressed with astonishing speed and ended up as directors, chief buyers or merchandise controllers before our 35th birthdays, with comfortable four-figure salaries and lush offices to boot.' But, like so many of *Cosmo*'s readers in the early seventies, Penny had received mixed messages about the possibilities open to young, female school leavers. Even while wanting to encourage young women away from dead-end jobs, school careers mistresses were ill-informed as to the opportunities opening up.

The Equal Pay Act (1970) had been designed to eliminate discrimination in pay between men and women, but didn't finally come into force until the end of 1975, alongside the Sex Discrimination Act, which made it unlawful to discriminate on grounds of sex or marital status, in promotion, recruitment and training. *Cosmopolitan* realised that these laws, though valuable, were not enough. It would take supreme confidence – and determination – to bring a case before the Equal Opportunities Commission. And at this point, even where opportunities for advancement existed, women were simply not putting themselves forward.

In May 1977 *Cosmopolitan* launched its Career Guide Service with the following impassioned introduction:

'Where do you see yourself in ten years from now?' asks the managing director of keen Mr Grey Flannel Suit who is being interviewed for the job of personal assistant. 'Sitting behind your desk,' promptly replies the young man, assuming the confident voice and intent expression which he has rehearsed so often since his Business Studies Self-Projection course and which he hopes is not betrayed by his trembling hand as he takes the cup of tea offered by the glacial Miss Smith. 'My admirable secretary' is the way she was introduced to him and later, when he arrived on his first day – yes, his bluff worked and he got the job – she is again introduced with cheery caution: 'Anything you want to know, ask Miss Smith. Marvellous girl! She runs the place.'

And probably she does, efficiently, effortlessly and unobtrusively. Indeed, she can handle most things and most people, except herself. The 'girl' is in her late twenties: she has been a senior secretary for several years and this is not the first young man she has seen stumble his way through a job she could do with her hands tied. But it's they who are promoted into management and she who remains behind to pick up the pieces and, in due course, induct yet another eager young hopeful, each time feeling a little more bitter and a lot more frustrated. But does she ever think of putting herself forward for the position? Of course not. She doesn't want to be dubbed aggressive or unfeminine and, besides, deep down she isn't convinced that she wants or could cope with the responsibility; it's one thing doing her own job, quite another to move into a position where she will be expected, among other things, to tell subordinates how to do theirs. No one has ever asked where she thinks she will be ten years from now and, to be honest, she doesn't care to think that far ahead; marriage and a family, a nice home, and a kind, protective husband she has always assumed to be her ultimate goal.

Miss Smith, super secretary; Mrs Jones, reliable and conscientious – an older woman taking a job she suspects is way beneath her capabilities, but glad of the money and the chance to escape from a home which was beginning to feel like a prison; and Mary Brown, straight out of school or college, who is keen to find work and start saving with the building society, but has no idea what she wants to do or where to start looking – three typical women who share one basic weakness in common with hundreds of other women, including, no doubt, some of you reading this article. It has never occurred to any of them to take themselves seriously as working women, to plan ahead for a future which will include an interesting, developing, well-paid job, regardless of whether they marry or have children. Almost certainly, their imagination has never leapt forward to consider the unthinkable – the prospect of being alone and possibly unsupported, with children to bring up and no qualifications or experience worth speaking of to fall back on.

The article went on to say that despite the imperfect and patchy laws on sex discrimination and equal pay, improvements in economic and family rights had made it easier for women to think about stepping out of the stereotypes prepared for them by traditional attitudes and expectations. New laws don't automatically change attitudes, it acknowledged, and people can't be forced to use them to their advantage unless they recognise them as relevant to their own circumstances. Women were still going to have to contend with their own conditioning: the desire to please and be pleasing, because that is how they were taught they would capture a man and charm friends and relations. The time had come to stop repressing ambition because 'girls don't or can't do the same things as boys.'

Cosmo readers were asked to fill in a questionnaire about their skills, current work and future aspirations. For a £5 administration fee, careers guidance expert Carolyn Faulder would give individually tailored advice, backed up by addresses and people to contact. Forget the G spot, *Cosmo* had discovered the readers' C spot – the place where career aspirations might actually be turned into reality.

The Working Woman section of *Cosmopolitan* was born – to explore career opportunities, but also new concepts like flexitime, networking and job-sharing. Its ambitions were to be far-reaching. In September 1979 *Cosmopolitan* had run a story about The Pepperell Development Course – a three-day developmental training aimed at encouraging women to develop their potential and achieve greater results at work.

The snag was that it cost £200. Generally the employer would pay. But not that many young women were working for bosses enlightened enough to send a bright young person of the female persuasion for training. So *Cosmo* linked up with Julia Cleverdon, who ran the Pepperell Courses, and offered readers a one-day programme for just £25. And in case anyone thought they were getting something second-rate, speakers on the course – all women who had great success in their chosen careers – included the newscaster Anna Ford and a half dozen other high-flyers. 'Change your life one Saturday' ran the magazine's banner headline – and thousands rushed to do just that.

To keep pace with the response, *Cosmo* began to offer more and more workshops and appointed Rachel Shattock (later to become *Cosmopolitan*'s deputy editor) to run them. The repertoire expanded to include training days dedicated to everything from getting jobs in TV, radio and PR to learning to be stress-free, make a pop video, public speaking, assertiveness training and running your own business.

Editor Deirdre McSharry, meanwhile, had fallen in love – with a little piece of equipment called the word processor. Determined to be the first major magazine to abolish the typewriter for its staff, she was equally determined that the readers of *Cosmopolitan* would sign up for the brave new world of technology. 'Love it or Luddite it,' she enthused in her editor's letter in 1981, 'the word processor is with us. Installed at last in our office, it hums like a contented hive, the copy flowing like honey. Visitors flock in from rival mags for an envious glance. People stand around fascinated ... I can just see number one on the bestseller list: *Sex and the Single Word-Processor*. The next problem will be to stop the staff treating the word-processor as a pet with gifts of plants and cards.

'Anyone who has been on one of the *Cosmo*-sponsored introductory courses to the mighty word-processor, will agree that the technological revolution is here to stay,' Deirdre continued, 'and as this one has women in the vanguard it will be fascinating to see what we do with our new power.' Deirdre was spot-on about the new technology, but, as for women being in the vanguard, that turned out to be just wishful thinking.

> 'Forget the G spot, Cosmo *had* discovered the readers' C spot – the place where career aspirations might actually be turned into reality.'

When actress Melanie Griffiths purred that she had 'a head for business and a bod for sin,' (in the 1988 movie *Working Girl*), *Cosmo* girls the world over inwardly cheered. The story of the 30-year-old single woman who, when her boss stole her bright idea, decided to perk up her sec's life (not to mention her sex life) and steal it right back again, was funny and empowering. The fact that her boss was a woman (played by Sigourney Weaver) was another modern eighties twist, an example of the Queen Bee syndrome, as explained on the pages of *Cosmopolitan*. Queen Bees, we told our readers, were women who, despite making it to the top feel their grip on power to be so tenuous that they block the path to success for other women. Even in the eighties, the 'sisterhood' had its bad days.

And so to shoulder pads. Fashion as the ultimate weapon in the sex war. Rather embarrassed though I feel when I look back on it, the minute I put on my pillar-box red, nipped-in-at-the-waist, Lolita Lempicka jacket that made me look like a cross between Joan Collins in *Dynasty* and Will Carling as he strutted onto the pitch, I felt in control and in charge. Getting wedged in narrow doorways was a small price to pay for such a convincing carapace of confidence. Yes, we were obsessed with work in the eighties, and with good reason in a workplace in which women were still routinely sexually harassed and discriminated against.

Writing in 1992, on the twentieth anniversary of *Cosmopolitan*, Naomi Miller reflected on the huge changes that had taken place in the twenty years since *Cosmo* had launched.

> Given the option to travel between 1972 and 1992, I'd take the present every time. I'd scoop up friends from the past and carry them forward on the nearest cross-chronological charabanc. I remember 1972 – just – and I don't look back in anger but I do remember it as an unsatisfying time for women, hovering between the pre-sixties doll's house and the real world of today.

She went on to describe the changes in women's lives, as single women, wives, mothers, and in the workplace:

> We may look back with some shame and horror on the eighties as greedily given over to making money. But at least that money came from our efforts – which is better than marrying it. Now, young women refuse to waste time waiting for a man to come along and rescue them. They know from the start that they must take charge of their own lives and forge a career – their own, not his.
>
> As for women's careers, although there are few women in parliament today (44), in 1972 there were only 24 female MPs … and there wasn't an executive skirt or shoulder pad to be seen in the City. The idea of networking – women getting together to exchange ideas, contacts and improve their working status – was alien. We didn't know then what we

could achieve or how powerful we could be as vehicles for change.

… You can begin life as an ordinary girl and grow up to be Tracy Edwards, sailing around the world. You can start off as a buyer of underwear in Marks & Spencer and end up with your own chain of stores and a multi-million turnover like Janie Godber of Knickerbox. You can have a family, a supportive husband and edit a national newspaper, like Eve Pollard at the *Sunday Express*.

You can be Helen Sharman – the first British person in space. Today, even the sky isn't the limit …

In the same twentieth anniversary issue, under the headline, 'What We Want Now', the magazine outlined its women's agenda for the nineties.

From the mid-nineties, with *Cosmo* under the editorship of Mandi Norwood, the magazine set out to re-define success for a new generation of twenty-somethings. The 'greed is good' ethic of the eighties, summed up by Oliver Stone's 1987 movie *Wall Street* and the wake-up call of the economic crash of the same year, turned ambition into something of a dirty word. Images of women with their brief-cases, shoulder-pads and killer heels came to represent a fearsome breed of voracious, success-at-any-price, super-bitches. Erica Jong announced that the most lasting legacy of liberation would be 'women's right to feel terminally exhausted.' And as for Having It All, Doing It All

'We may look back with shame on the eighties as greedily given over to making money. But at least that money came from our efforts – which is better than marrying it.'

was starting to sound a more accurate description. No wonder women were becoming to feel a bit ambivalent about ambition and where it would lead.

So in 1997, Mandi Norwood's *Cosmo* introduced a newly-packaged version of ambition. The new ambition, the magazine ambitiously declared, was 'friendly, flexible and fun …'

'Ambition – the desire to succeed' ran the introduction to the magazine's working girl special:

If you think of it in those terms, you'd be crazy *not* to be ambitious. Having ambition is another way of saying you have aspirations, drive and energy. You want to fulfil your dreams – whatever they may be.

You may wish to be prime minister or to be big in the City, travel the world, marry a great lover, have six children, live in a cottage in the country, invent a cure for the common cold … Someone will do one, two or all of these things – why not you?

That's the point. Nineties ambition is about sorting out what you want, what, for *you*, equals success. So, your goals won't make you a million? It doesn't detract from their validity. In the eighties, 'ambition' became entangled with greed – for money, power, fast cars, Fogal tights. If you were greedy for happiness, for fulfilment, you weren't ambitious – you were a sap. In 1997, ambition can mean different things to different people. You can be ambitious for a high-flying career. You can be ambitious for personal happiness. You can be ambitious for a charitable cause.

> '*Ambition gives your life extra vroom! It makes you bounce out of bed in the morning. It imbues your life with passion and hope.*'

Whatever your ambition, the point is to acknowledge it and make it work for you. Ambition is, after all, what gives your existence that extra *vroom*! It makes you bounce out of bed in the morning. It imbues your life with passion and hope. Whatever your wildest dream, you owe it to yourself to pursue it – and succeed.

In 2002, *Cosmo* still waves the occasional banner for women at work, although features like 'Get a Cosmic Career Boost' in which *Cosmo* astrologer Sarah Bartlett 'reveals the celestial secrets that will help you shine in the workplace,' suggest that not only has the glass ceiling been shattered, now you can head straight for the stars. The truth is more discomfiting. In the month following *Cosmo*'s 30th anniversary celebrations, the Equal Opportunities Commission announced the results of research that proves pay parity and sex equality in the workplace are complete myths. Male graduates, aged 24, earn 15 per cent more than female graduates in the same occupations who have achieved the same class of degree in the same subjects. For 30-year-olds, the graduate pay gap is 22 per cent, rising to a 38 per cent difference at age 40 and 44 per cent difference at age 50. A likely explanation, said Carl Gilleard, chief executive of the Assocation of Graduate Recruiters, which represents 500 leading companies, was secrecy about pay levels. In other words, women are offered less than men – and they accept it. You've may have come a long way, baby, but you've still got a helluva way to go.

MAKING IT WORK

1975 Parliament enacts the **Sex Discrimination Act** which goes into effect simultaneously with the **Equal Pay Act.** Discrimination on the grounds of gender or marital status, in recruitment, training, promotion or pay is now illegal.

1976 Anita Roddick opens her first **Body Shop** in Brighton. Green is good, women declared, and a multi-million pound business was born.

1979 Margaret Thatcher becomes Britain's first female Prime Minister.

1980 National Childcare Campaign is set up to lobby for improved childcare facilities for the increasing numbers of women going out to work.

1980 The 300 Group is founded and aims for 50 per cent female representation in Parliament.

1986 In the case of Strathclyde Regional Council vs Mrs Porcelli, sexual harassment was clearly regarded as a form of sexual discrimination for the first time.

1987 In another landmark case of Ms White and others vs Alstons (Colchester) Ltd, female machinists were held to be engaged in work of equal value to male upholsterers and awarded equal pay.

1990 Women are allowed to be **taxed separately** from their husbands.

1991 Ex-dancer, Betty Boothroyd, becomes the first woman Speaker of the House of Commons.

1992 **Stella Rimington** becomes the first female Director of MI5.

1994 The **first female Anglican priests** are ordained at Bristol Cathedral.

1996 In a sex discrimination case, **2000 dinner ladies** in Cleveland are awarded a £1 million payout, following a claim against their employer, Cleveland County Council.

2003 Women are awarded six months' paid and six months' unpaid maternity leave in an **Employment Bill** due to come into force in 2004.

2003 From April 2003 employers will be obliged to give serious consideration to a reduction or change in working hours for working parents of children under the age of six.

WOMEN ON THE JOB

• In 2000, 25 years after the Sex Discrimination and Equal Pay Acts came into force, women still received just 74 per cent of men's average weekly earnings.

• In 1974, women made up 1.8 per cent of all executives (i.e. directors and managers) according to the National Management Salary Survey. By 2000, this figure had risen to 22.1 per cent.

• In 2002, according to the Female FTSE Report, women make up just 3 per cent of executive directors in the top 100 firms, and just 7 per cent of board of directors. There are still 39 firms in the top 100 without a single woman on the board.

• Women barristers practising at the independent bar in England and Wales, up from 7 per cent in 1975 to 26 per cent in 2000.

• Women engineers still comprised just 2 per cent of registered engineers at the end of 1999.

• In 1974 there were 27 women MPs. In 2001 the number had increased to 118.

RICH CHICKS – THE ONES WHO KNOW THEY'RE WORTH IT

Of the 500 people in The Pay List 2002, *The Sunday Times* guide to the UK's biggest earners, only 59 women featured.

• Top female earner of the year, with a cool £36 million, was Madonna, included because of her London home and marriage to Brit film director Guy Ritchie. Other rich rock chicks on the list were Dido, Kylie, Sade and new entries Sonique and Sophie Ellis-Bextor.

• Seven of the top ten earners in the world of fashion were models – including Alex Wek, Vivien Solari, Karen Elson and Erin O'Connor. The poorest top ten model this year was pregnant Kate Moss who notched up a mere £2.35 million. Rose Marie Bravo of Burberry made £2.8 million.

• The write stuff – but only if you're a J K Rowling, Barbara Taylor Bradford or Jackie Collins. J K's £28 million earnings sandwiched her pay packet neatly between that of Madonna and Catherine Zeta-Jones.

• Media babes made buckets including Anne Robinson (£6.25 million), Liz Hurley (£2.15 million – down from £3.94 million the previous year – for her varied dabblings in modelling, acting and producing) and Carol Vordemann who counted up £2.8 million. Cilla Black was still raking it in, too, with £2 million.

• Acting to the hilt was Catherine Zeta-Jones, £14–15 million richer by the end of 2002. Rachel Weisz made masses of money from *Confidence*, *Entry*, *About a Boy* and a deal with Revlon, amassing £3.5 million.

• Business babes included Stella Andreou and Eleni Pishiris, whose share in the family food business netted each of them £16.32 million. Barbara Cassani, the only woman ever to have run an airline, made a pretty packet, pocketing £9.5 million when Go was sold to EasyJet.

CHAPTER 6

YOU'RE GORGEOUS

Cosmopolitan **has never** been primarily a fashion and beauty magazine, although over the years those elements have become an increasingly important part of the mix. Today readers expect more – and advertisers also expect to see greater coverage of the fashion and beauty products they produce. The fashion in *Cosmo* now provides a real service to the readers. Still sexy, still glamorous, still fun, but useful too, and there's much more of it. The 30th anniversary issue carried over 60 pages of fashion and beauty, more than enough to rival the other glossies.

In the early days *Cosmo*'s fashion was very much an extension of the magazine's features, with the emphasis on dressing for seduction, or dressing to please your man, often with hilarious results. Male models smouldered in the background, nuzzled necks or just hung around draped in a tiny towel. The girls favoured evening dresses and underwear, nothing so practical as what to wear for work or the weekend. Thematic stories like 'Confessions Of An Underwear Freak', complete with camp, self-parodying pictures of a girl greeting the milkman/postman/florist/plumber in her bra and panties ran alongside witty little ditties such as those shown overleaf:

'I like to be up before the birds,
And be ready to take in the milk.
Actions always speak louder than words,
So I dress for the milkman in silk.'

In 1972, **Cosmo** fashion featured sexy underwear and slinky party dresses – but nothing so practical as what to wear for work or the weekend.

'He sends me roses, red as sin,
 My old and fat adorer;
But as the florist's young and thin,
 I'm really inter flora!'

Celebrities featured strongly on the fashion pages. A jeans-update story starred Charlotte Rampling, Joanne Lumley and Britt Ekland and welcomed the new approach to jeans design for women. 'The likely lads at Levis (who have been selling jeans since 1848) and elsewhere, are keeping the sales soaring this summer with an extra ingredient – sex,' wrote the magazine's first fashion editor Deirdre McSharry, in May 1972. 'Noting that one of the essential differences between the sexes is the gap at the back of the waist caused by the pear-shaped female bottom, jeans manufacturers are plugging that gap with specially shaped and seamed jeans that cling round the bottom and flare at the hem …'

Some fashions never die. In September 1972 *Cosmo* interviewed and photographed Bianca Jagger, exotic new Nicaraguan wife of Rolling Stone Mick. She arrived at the studio accompanied by 'a coffin-sized Vuitton case … and shoemaker Manolo of Zapata with two dozen pairs of four-inch high heel shoes.' Celebrity style-watchers should find this particular snippet of fashion history fascinating. In 2002 the shoemaker of choice for A-list celebrities is *still* Manolo Blahnik – Sarah Jessica Parker, star of *Sex and the City,* recently gushed, 'I feel honoured that I will be able to say to my grandchildren, "I met Manolo Blahnik and I owned some of his shoes".' And no Hollywood star would dream of travelling without her entourage of Vuitton suitcases.

In May 1976, *Cosmo* introduced Bianca's successor, Jerry Hall, to the fashion pages of *Cosmopolitan.* 'Bottoms out,' the magazine declared, as Jerry draped herself provocatively over a hunky male model's thigh. Helen Mirren, meanwhile, showed herself to be pure *Cosmo* girl by declaring 'I dress to look sexy and raise a laugh. I wear stockings and suspenders, *not* tights.'

Celebrities featured strongly on the fashion pages. Bianca Jagger, Joanna Lumley, Britt Ekland and Charlotte Rampling all did star turns in the early editions.

Back in the seventies even liberated *Cosmo* girls still sometimes reached for the sewing machine. Patterns featured regularly in the magazine. And fur-consciousness had not yet been raised as 6ft model Veruschka demonstrated when she posed, in 1974, in the ultimate decadent combination – luscious leather and sumptuous fur.

If looking gorgeous was always a priority for the *Cosmo* girl, getting fit was not – in the early seventies – high up on the agenda. Aerobics hadn't been invented and the nearest the *Cosmo* girl got to working out was running for the bus. Still, we made a stab at encouraging the reader to shape up in March 1972, with a pictorial guide to office exercising. Stretching out to pick up paper clips, we told the reader, would be effective in countering sit-down spread. Banging a filing cabinet closed with your bottom, we advised, would firm the buttocks (never mind the bruising!).

Dieting, rather than exercising, was very much in vogue. No. 1 diet guru of the day was Dr Atkins with his revolutionary new low carbohydrate diet, as featured in the March 1972 issue of *Cosmopolitan*. Described as a bachelor with a passion for pretty girls and good food, Dr Atkins banned all fruit for those following his diet. 'I see pretty girls – a little too plump, but pretty – taking their lunch to the park. And what do they have? Three pieces of fruit. There is a false assumption that fruit has no calories … or very few. It not only has the calories, but it's loaded with carbohydrates.' But two eggs for breakfast, fried in butter, were OK. Today, Dr Atkins' New Diet Revolution, published at the end of the 1990s, is widely reported to be followed by Whoopi Goldberg, Jennifer Aniston, Geri Halliwell and Renee Zelwegger, amongst many other celebrities. It is back on the bestseller lists, having sold more than 3 million copies worldwide, and is still promoting that early seventies favourite, the low-carbohydrate diet.

'Dieter's Notebook' was a popular regular feature of the early seventies and celebrities were happy to pass on their secrets for successful slimming. 'Falling in love,' declared Jilly Cooper, 'is the way to lose weight – I've been known to lose 8 lbs. Or perhaps having a husband who's foul enough to say you're fat.' Romantic novelist Barbara Cartland disapproved of slimming on the basis that 'most men like a handful'. But for those who insisted on slimming, she suggested, 'One egg for breakfast, a spoonful of honey, one apple, a cup of weak tea, two multi-vitamin tablets (vitamin E for women) and four bone-meal tablets a day. Meat and vegetables for both lunch and dinner. One spoonful of honey at tea-time and again at night to make you sleep well. The meat is impor-tant: after all you've never seen a fat tigress. It's a crashing bore, your husband will run away with a blonde, but you'll be slim ...' Newspaper columnist Katherine Whitehorn suggested the Gin Diet, her own invention, which involved eating very little but perking yourself up after putting the kids to bed with gin and unsweetened grapefruit juice.

Joanna Lumley advised ordering anything you like in a restaurant and making a great show of enjoying yourself. 'Munch away,' she told the readers, 'but only eat one mouthful.' Harry Secombe, the rotund Welshman, had the best advice of all 'Eat as much as you like but don't swallow it. I've lost pounds that way.'

In March 1978, with the publication of Susie Orbach's *Fat Is A Feminist Issue, Cosmo*'s love-affair with dieting ended. It was hard not to be swayed by Susie's passionate and coherent argument that over-weight women were using their 'fatness' as a way to protect themselves from their sexuality and that the diet-binge syndrome could be overcome by learning the difference between stomach hunger (when you needed to eat) and mouth hunger (when you were eating to feed a psychological rather than physical need). The goal, as described by Susie, was 'not primarily weight loss. The goal is for the compulsive eater to break her addictive relationship towards food. While weight loss is generally an important sign that the addiction is broken, our primary concern is that you begin to feel more comfortable about food.' Having reported on Susie Orbach's findings, *Cosmo*'s 'Dieter's Notebook' feature was quickly dropped.

In the same year, *Cosmo* discovered the health and fitness craze that was taking California by storm, and adopted it as its own, 'Even if – indeed, espe-cially if – you work sitting behind your typewriter or hugging the phone it must be apparent that a new age is dawning – The Age of Health. Gymnasts, dancers and footballers are the current heroes; health-food nuts are listened to respectfully and every office has its own jogger boasting how many laps she ran that morning. At lunchtime there's a lemming-like rush to pool or park for the midday exercise fix ... Whether you see yourself as the local Farrah Fawcett-Majors or the office Olga Korbut, or you just want to walk up 76 stairs without puffing, the only person who can motivate you to fitness is yourself.

*Jerry Hall was a **Cosmo** favourite in the seventies.*

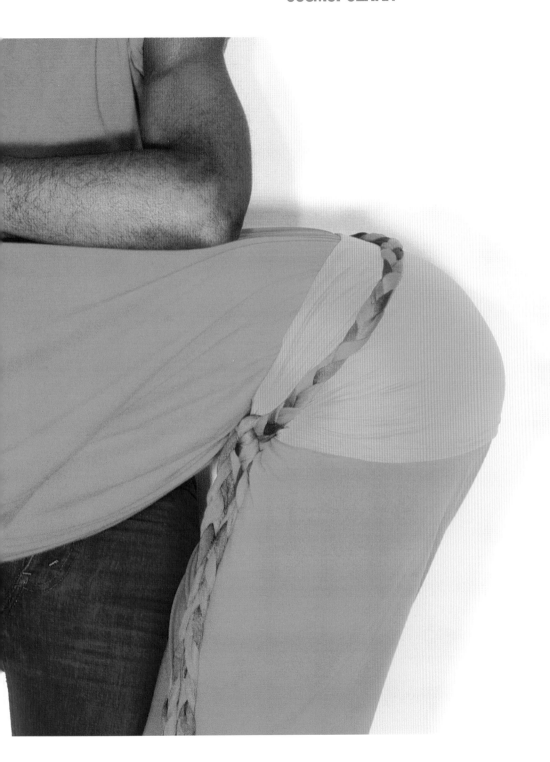

Experts agree that those who wish to live the healthy life should find a diet that suits them, avoid stress and be realistic about exercise. Do what comes naturally – while jogging is fashionable, you might enjoy a dance class more.'

At around the same time *Cosmopolitan* launched the first of its 'Shape Tapes,' available by mail order to the readers:

It's funky, it's fun and will keep you as lithe as a professional dancer,' the magazine promised. 'Switch on the *Cosmopolitan* Shape Tape the moment you wake up in the morning and launch into a ten to fifteen minute work-out that will make you feel fitter, slimmer and more energetic than ever before. The routine (adapted from the jazz dancing course at the world-famous Dance Centre by choreographer Arlene Phillips) will have you bending and stretching and toning up every muscle you have, plus quite a few you never knew existed.

Thousands of readers couldn't wait to get their hands on the *Cosmopolitan* Shape Tape and the numerous other exercise tapes that followed it.

In 1979 *Cosmo* readers were introduced to Pilates, two decades before it became the hot way to shape up that it is today. And in May 1983, *Zest* – a special, regular section dedicated to health and fitness – was added on to the magazine. At that time editor Deirdre McSharry had been keen to launch *Zest* as a spin-off magazine in its own right, but not until 1994 were the board of directors convinced that the health and fitness boom was here to stay and that a glossy magazine dedicated to fitness and well-being could survive. In the meantime *Zest* swelled sales of *Cosmopolitan* throughout the eighties as a regular, banded supplement to the magazine.

In January 1997, *Cosmopolitan* launched its new year health special with a feature entitled 'What A Fit Body Really Looks Like'. The California blonde supermodels of the early eighties, like the impossibly gorgeous Christie Brinkley, all teeth, smiles and big hair, were no longer the kind of role models to which the readers aspired. Now *Cosmo* girls were doing it for themselves as the seven real readers photographed for the feature – fabulously fit and not a weight-obsessive among them – demonstrated. But of course no sooner has one obsession been conquered than another one starts battling for supremacy. Watch out for 'orthorexia', *Cosmo* warned in September 1998. 'Whereas anorexics focus on quantity of food, orthorexics concentrate on quality,' said Dr Steve Bratman, a nutrition specialist. 'Orthorexics, the magazine reported, are the increasing number of young, female health-nuts who extol the virtues of healthy eating, but end up jeopardising their health because of a fixation about allergies, yeast problems or only eating raw foods.

In a recent issue *Cosmopolitan* dedicated a special report to Emotional Eating Syndrome. Susie Orbach was once again consulted. 'You may think a double chocolate-chip muffin is just what you need to put that row with your boyfriend out of your head, when what you really need is a hug and reassurance that he still loves you.'

So is the *Cosmopolitan* reader today healthier, fitter, less weight-obsessed than the reader who picked up *Cosmo* 30 years ago? Women generally, it seems, are getting bigger. In 1972 the average bust/waist/hip measurements were around 35in/27in/37in. These days women measure in at 36.5in/30in/39.5in. And the predictions for *Cosmo's* 60th anniversary? According to Philip Treleaven, Deputy Head of Computer Science at University College, London, who is currently compiling a National Sizing Survey, women's bust size will increase to 37-38in, waist to 30-32in and hips to 39-40in. Women are getting taller, too, heading towards an average of 5ft 5in and a weight of just under 10 stone. One in five women in the UK is currently obese, according to the National Audit Office. Philip Treleaven says we're eating more and exercising less. Meanwhile, gym membership is soaring. But as *Cosmo* readers are well aware, joining the gym and going to the gym are two completely different propositions.

All fashion goes in cycles and it's probably mere chance that the hot looks for summer 2002 perfectly reflected what every girl wanted to wear exactly 30 years earlier. But for *Cosmo* celebrating its 30th birthday, it was a neat coincidence. Wedges were everywhere, peasant-tops dominated both

'Today's Cosmo reader is dressing first and foremost to please herself.'

designer-wear and the high street, floaty chiffon frocks abounded. Vintage Ossie Clarks (as worn by Bianca Jagger in *Cosmo*) became the most coveted buys of summer 2002. Hippie met the new millennium and looked back in languor. But there was one big difference. If the original *Cosmo* girl was dressing purely to please her man, today's *Cosmo* reader is dressing first and foremost to please herself. And you can't deny that's progress.

CHAPTER 7

THE BIG ISSUES

From promoting sexual health and equal pay, to exposing sexual harassment and domestic violence, *Cosmopolitan* has always championed the causes that women care about, and campaigned vigorously on their behalf. Looking back through the *Cosmo* archive, I think it would be fair to say that no other women's magazine in the past 30 years has come close to *Cosmo* in its ongoing coverage of the issues that are central to women's well-being. While *Marie Claire* may have combed the world to seek out injustices in Eritrea or Iran, *Cosmo* has always found plenty to shout about on its own doorstep.

In 1972 it was a brave woman who, despite the knowledge that abortion had been legal since 1968, actually admitted to having had one. *Cosmopolitan*'s stance on the subject, 'Why The Abortion Law Doesn't Work', provoked unsurprising outburst from the 'pro-life' lobby – and grateful agreement from the majority of readers. In 2002 few women in the UK would find an abortion difficult to obtain or feel stigmatised for having had one. But as far as many of the other central issues are concerned, there's been no such progress.

Take *Cosmo*'s passion for safe, or at least 'safer' sex, for example. It was in 1987, when everyone was terrified of AIDS, that *Cosmo* first declared, 'Smart girls carry condoms'. And it was June 2001 when Lorraine Candy, *Cosmo*'s current editor, endorsed the new *Cosmo* Condom Campaign with the following injunction:

> Are you an intelligent woman? A modern woman, independent and confident? Of course you are, and I applaud you. But many of you are doing something monumentally stupid, that risks your health, your fertility and perhaps your life. You are having unprotected sex … Here at *Cosmo*, we're all for a healthy, happy, adventurous sex life. We don't condemn one-night stands, casual sex or sex with different partners. Whatever makes you feel good about yourself is fine with us. But it's a different matter if you don't value yourself.
>
> Women we talked to gave several reasons why they don't use condoms. Too shy to buy them, too tipsy to remember, too embarrassed to negotiate 'the condom moment'. These are women like you – bright, articulate, self-sufficient – yet they couldn't understand the concept of safe sex.
>
> In fact, I'd say they're more worried about what he thinks of their body shape than catching a sexually transmitted infection. But the priorities here are so wrong. If you value yourself, take one simple step – buy condoms.

In 1971, Erin Pizzey, who became a regular contributor to *Cosmopolitan* and wrote often on the subject of domestic violence, opened the first refuge for women in West London. Throughout the seventies, eighties and nineties, domestic violence was a subject to which the magazine returned, with particular emphasis on the difficulties women faced in getting up and leaving violent men, the indifference shown by the police when domestic violence was finally reported, and the need for greater government intervention.

In November 2001, under the banner 'Stop. In the name of love', *Cosmo* introduced its campaign to put a stop to the threat of emotional and physical violence in the home with a thirteen-page report and an introduction from Cherie Booth QC, who's a trustee of the charity Refuge:

Dear *Cosmo* Reader, *Cosmo*'s support of Refuge and this campaign to end domestic violence is more important than you perhaps imagine. Too few of us realise this is one issue which is sure to touch us all. When one woman out of four is abused in her lifetime, the stark truth is that even if you are not abused yourself, you know someone who has been or will be. Unless we all face up to this fact, our friends, our colleagues, our relatives – women we know and love – will continue to suffer in silence.

When I started out on my legal career, I often found myself representing women who had been abused. I was shocked to see them arrive at court with bruises, scars or missing teeth, and with their esteem in tatters. It was even more distressing when they had been beaten while pregnant or when the violence had taken place in front of their children …

She went on to describe how 30 years ago, *Cosmo* and Refuge began to give women a voice, a voice that over the years has become louder, and she emphasised the continuing need to speak out.

To illustrate *Cosmo*'s coverage of the big issues I could have chosen pieces about power or the Pill; screening for cervical cancer or the behaviour of judges in rape cases; the importance of being financially independent or how, for many people, friends have replaced families. I've limited myself, for reasons of space, to 'a big issue' from each decade. What the 1972 abortion story tells us is how women were, for the first time, beginning to take charge of their own reproductive fate (abetted also by the Pill). 'No sex ads, we're British', written in the early eighties, pointed out government hypocrisy in relation to sex education. In 1992, the backlash against the monstrous regiment of eighties career women was in full force – and *Cosmo* set out to counter it with Melissa Benn's powerfully argued 'Brace Yourself for the Backlash'. By 2001, *Cosmo* had gone full circle on the issue of domestic violence, but with some progress. Just as in 1972 a roll-call of celebrated women had the courage to speak out about abortion, 30 years later, a small but growing number of well-known women had the courage to go public about domestic violence. *Cosmo*'s report included the brave voices of Martine McCutcheon and pop star Missy Elliott, both of whom had witnessed their mothers being beaten by their fathers.

Why the abortion law doesn't work

Alice Lynn Booth
March 1972

'You wouldn't think that abortion is legal in this country – not with all the manoeuvring and secrecy.'

Louise, the 22-year old mother of three young children, sighed with relief as she perched herself up on her brightly covered bed six hours after her abortion:

'I have a boy of two and twins, four months old. I couldn't cope with another child either financially or emotionally. Yet, my GP wouldn't discuss my pregnancy with me. Fortunately, I knew about the local Family Planning Association and they recommended the Birmingham Pregnancy Advisory Service. But still I feel underhanded and embarrassed about it all. My GP made such a secret of it – I felt as if I was asking for something quite illegal.'

Louise is one of 72,109 women (out of 126,774) who, during 1971, had her abortion notified as being performed in a private licensed nursing home. Discouraged by her GP, Louise found her way to the Birmingham Pregnancy Advisory Service (BPAS), a charity trust with a nursing home in Brighton, Sussex. In only a week, and less than twelve weeks pregnant, Louise arrived at Wiston's Nursing Home where for a £6 consulting fee, a £45 operating charge and a round-trip ticket, she had an abortion in cheerful, immaculate surroundings. Still, she felt confused. 'A doctor shouldn't hold back information.

WHY THE ABORTION LAW DOESN'T WORK

Abortion became legal in this country in 1968, but anyone who expected that termination would become as easy as tonsillectomy has been sadly disillusioned. True, the Act has averted numbers of tragedies and prevented thousands of unwanted children being born, but for many women, and for all sorts of reasons, it simply doesn't work. It doesn't work because:

● Unsympathetic doctors often make girls feel embarrassed, ashamed or even as if they have committed a crime.

● A girl who decides quite rationally that she wants a termination frequently has to put on a great show of hysteria to convince a gynaecologist or psychiatrist.

● Lack of facilities and co-ordination often result in decisions being delayed until termination is very dangerous or no longer possible.

● Difficulties in obtaining NHS abortions mean that those with the knowhow and the cash to have private treatment have preference over less fortunate women who may well be in greater need.

These problems can only be solved by a vast increase in facilities for abortion and by the acceptance that every woman who wants an abortion should be allowed to have one. Abortion on demand is a very sensitive subject. The anti-lobby will talk about religious implications, will argue that the life of the foetus is sacred, that abortion is psychologically damaging and that the girl who is refused an abortion will afterwards be grateful. These are such powerful arguments that surely every woman has the right to work them out for herself and decide what she wants to do with *her own body* and *her own life*. This is our opinion, and many well-known women agree with us and feel strongly enough to allow their views to appear in print (see overleaf). We admire their courage.

THESE WOMEN HAVE HAD ABORTIONS

 Buzz Goodbody
 Maxine Audley
 Shirley Ann Field
 Joan Heal
 Lelia Goldoni

 Georgia Brown
 Ann Lynn
 Melissa Stribling
 Ann Firbank
 Patricia Cutts

31

I hadn't the slightest idea that a place like Wiston's existed.'

Despite Louise's disturbing impression, abortion is most certainly legal in Britain. Since the Abortion Act went into effect in April 1968, a total of 288,234 pregnancy terminations have been notified. British women don't have to fear criminal prosecution for having abortions nor should they need to search out abortionists in back alleys. They no longer have to feign suicidal wishes to indifferent psychiatrists. Still, getting an abortion in Britain isn't quite the same as having an appendix removed. Girls who succeed have to display strong fortitude and a good degree of resourcefulness. And they must face a social climate that still considers abortion an unpleasant word – even a dirty one.

More than a third of the women whose pregnancies were terminated last year paid from £100 to £200 for this in private clinics; many had to suffer hostility and moralising lectures from GPs and gynaecologists, and even worse, for some the operation was delayed (either deliberately by a hostile doctor or because of waiting lists and complicated procedures in NHS hospitals) until it constituted a medical risk. Why? Because the government has made no provision to cope with the increasing demand for abortions and because the Abortion Act itself is vague and in the words of one gynaecologist – 'asks the doctor to be both judge and jury.'

For a pregnancy to be terminated, two doctors must state in good faith that continuing the pregnancy would involve risk to the life of the woman, or injury to her physical or mental health or injury to her existing children, greater than if she had an abortion (or that there is substantial risk that the child, when born, would be seriously handicapped).

According to Miss Dorothea Kerslake, medical director of the Fairfield Nursing Home in Woodford, Essex, the wording of the act implies that if it is 'better' for the patient to have an abortion than to have the child – because of medical, social or emotional reasons – then an abortion is permissible. 'In actual fact, termination is always safer than a full pregnancy. With termination, particularly in the first twelve weeks, we know the risks. With a full term pregnancy we can't foresee what may occur."

The Birmingham and London Pregnancy Advisory Services refer for abortions about 95 per cent of the women who come to them. These charity organisations offer abortions for £45 to £60 to girls who either can't get NHS abortions or don't want to try and who would have difficulty affording the high fees charged by private clinics. Both services watch for a patient's ambivalence before referring her for an abortion. 'We wish to protect women who shouldn't have abortions,' says BPAS's forceful director, Nan Smith. 'We want to be sure the decision is her own.' LPAS director, Myra Gainsly, puts it this way: 'We don't offer abortion on demand. We do offer relief to women who are distressed about unwanted pregnancies. If the distress is caused by the pregnancy, the best way to relieve the distress is to remove the pregnancy.'

Not all doctors take a liberal approach, however. Mrs G, a 31-year-old woman, explained her NHS gynaecologist's attitude: 'He said another child could leave me paralysed. Yet, when I asked him for an abortion he said the risk was 50/50 and I should take the risk. When I said I wasn't willing to risk it, he refused anyway.'

Mrs G's pretty nineteen-year-old room-mate at Wiston's was a university student with 'little money and no plans to marry'. Her GP told her she should get married and was healthy enough to have the baby. 'Then he berated me about getting pregnant.'

Nan Smith knew of one doctor who refused to terminate the pregnancy of a twelve-year-old girl. 'If a doctor has a moral or religious objection to abortion, he ceases to see each case individually. It all becomes very inhuman.'

The Secretary of the Royal College of Gynaecologists, Mr Edward Alment, believes the law is 'unjust and divisive'. 'What many women think the law means is quite the contrary to what many doctors think it means. Thus, the act is being interpreted in all sorts of ways and many women are left confused and with a sense of genuine injustice.'

Even though Mrs G described Wiston's as 'a lovely place where doctors put you at your ease,' she felt she had been treated unfairly. The total cost of her abortion reached £75 with train fares for her and her husband and hotel costs. 'Why should I have to travel and pay anything at all? Why couldn't I go to my local hospital? Certainly, I would go there to have a child.'

What Mrs G and thousands of other women have discovered is that having a free NHS abortion depends on the arbitrary fact of where the woman lives. In certain parts of London, in Southern Wales, and in Newcastle, for example, where doctors are sympathetic to abortion or have a good number of beds in relation to population, a genuinely distressed woman can be fairly sure of getting an NHS abortion with little inconvenience. In other places, particularly Birmingham, Liverpool and Manchester, where the gynaecologists have rigid attitudes and bed spaces may be more limited, the same woman would have considerably less chance of having an NHS abortion.

Diane Munday, general secretary of the Abortion Law Reform Society, believes that most hospitals are too rigid about allocating beds for specific purposes. 'If a woman doesn't have an abortion, she is going to have a baby. I'd like to know how the NHS would cope with about 127,000 added births a year. Hospitals could transfer maternity beds to gynaecological wards – especially now that we have a falling birthrate. I think this is a lovely convenient excuse for refusing abortions.'

The British Medical Society recently proposed that 'adequate staff, beds and other amenities for all women entitled to abortions under the Act, and who wished the operation to be carried out under the NHS, must therefore be provided.' No one knows how much it would cost the NHS to do all the abortions in the country. Actually, if all of the 250 practising gynaecologists performed six a week, all the women now having abortions would get them in NHS hospitals. Even with added facilities and staff, however, Mr Alment doubts that an equitable distribution of abortion cases throughout the country could ever be realised.

'The attitude of gynaecologists towards abortion is such that many women would be denied abortions. In a recent survey of gynaecologists, only six per cent said they had an absolute conscientious objection to abortion in all circumstances. But 92 per cent said they would oppose abortion on demand. Therefore, a good number of gynaecologists wouldn't agree that all the women having abortions actually qualify under the law.'

Not everyone believes an NHS hospital is the best place for an abortion anyway. Before she can get there a girl must consult her GP. Not all women are willing to do this – either they feel ashamed about getting pregnant and don't want the family doctor to know or they fear he'll tell their families. Others assume he'll be hostile and don't want to add salt to an already painful wound. GP's have been known to deceive women into delaying termination or into going through with childbirth.

If a woman does get a bed in an NHS hospital, she may find the atmosphere less than amenable. 'She may share a room with a fertility treatment patient or a woman who's just had a miscarriage. Abortion patients are far better off in units or clinics where everyone shares the same predicament,' says Mrs Gainsly.

Even if the gynaecologist is sympathetic, a woman may face hostility from other members of the staff. 'A doctor must work with a team,' says Mr Alment. 'Sometimes nurses can be hostile to a patient and there is little the doctor can do about it.' A woman who called her NHS abortion 'the worst experience of my life' recalls a nurse presenting her with the foetus and screaming 'look what you have killed'. 'If I had to go through that again I wouldn't have the abortion,' said the woman.

Dr Malcolm Potts, a member of the London Pregnancy Advisory Service (LPAS) Management Committee, sees another drawback in NHS abortion. 'A patient gets far better medical treatment from a doctor who does only abortions than from one who does two abortions a day after a long day of other surgical procedures.'

Dr Potts is also extremely critical of the long delays that sometimes occur in the NHS system. 'A woman normally sees her GP when she is six to eight weeks pregnant. He refers her to the NHS hospital and that means a two-week wait. When she goes there the doctor tells her to wait until she misses another period. A week later he insists she sees a psychiatrist. By the time she has an appointment date (sometimes six weeks later), she is well over the twelve-week safety period and has to have an hysterectomy (cutting into the uterus through an abdominal incision). We're killing people because of this mishandling,' he says.

Dr Potts hopes that eventually women will have their abortions on an out-patient basis at a greatly reduced fee. At present nursing homes are required to keep patients for 24 hours as a safety factor and a means of controlling the number of patients who can be aborted in a day. A few London NHS hospitals are experimenting with out-patient abortions but the numbers they are able to deal with are very small and they are, of course, limited to women who live in their particular catchment area.

If a woman can't get an abortion through the National Health Service or doesn't want to try, where does she go? If she has £150 at her immediate disposal and someone tells her where to go to, she can take the first train to London and see a private doctor or go to one of the numerous private clinics in and around London. The Department of Health suggests women should go to a doctor who takes private patients, not direct to a nursing home.

Whether cost determines quality is highly questionable. 'We really know very little about the private clinics,' says Mr Alment. 'I do believe the Department of Health is pressurising them to improve their quality of care.' Mr Alment is sceptical, however, because 'the private clinics lie outside the traditional system of health care in England. If a woman isn't guided by her GP, she isn't going to get the guarantee an NHS patient has. It launches her into the unknown.'

Nan Smith believes that BPAS and LPAS fill the gap because they are non-profit charities created by an inadequate health service and a profiteering private sector. 'Our aim is to topple the private abortion scene,' says this strong-willed woman. 'I want to see all the rogues and robbers out of business.' According to Mrs Smith, the two charities with their three nursing homes (BPAS also sent patients to the Carthorpe Nursing Home in Birmingham where the fee is £60) are already catering to nearly half the private abortion patients in the country. 'We've already seen a good number of private clinics run out of business. No one can do a better job than we do.'

In its proposals to the Lane Committee (a committee investigating the workigns of the Abortion Act), LPAS suggested that the government set a maximum fee for abortions. 'Women have been exploited by the historical secretiveness of having abortions. The Act should have stopped this but it didn't,' says Mrs Sylvia Ponsonby, a member of the LPAS's Management Committee. 'The Department of Health should set a standard price for abortions.' LPAS also suggests government assistance to non-profitmaking abortion charities so they can establish more nursing homes and give grants to subsidise poor patients.

Having an abortion forces a girl to make an almost mind-shattering decision that requires deep soul searching. It means exposing herself to a series of medical examinations which she may find discomforting. It involves an operation that, although lasting only ten minutes (before twelve weeks), requires a general anaesthetic and brings the frightening awareness that her life is in another person's hands. And in this country where abortion still provokes shame and guilt, it can be a very lonely experience – particularly for a single girl. Most unmarried women hesitate to discuss this problem with even close friends and family. Having an abortion can mean going it alone, perhaps for the first time in a girl's life.

Because of the investigations of the Lane Committee, considered and badly needed attention is being focused on the entire abortion scene. The committee will report its findings in 1973 and make recommendations to Parliament. Hopefully, the government will be prodded into improving NHS abortion procedures and cleaning up the private abortion business.

Perhaps, the government will eliminate the vagueness of the law by adopting a law that permits abortion on demand. Only then will a woman have the right to determine when to have children. And only then will doctors be relieved of the impossible task of determining a woman's future health and happiness. A law that made the termination of her pregnancy a woman's right would finally end the guilt, shame and sordidness associated with abortion. And it would substantially reduce the opportunities for doctors to deceive and exploit women.

Meanwhile, thousands of women will continue to have their pregnancies terminated within the bounds of the law and the present system. Many will find that having an abortion today in Britain requires strong determination and a strong ego. Some will discover that having an abortion is an experience better forgotten but not always easy to forget.

'By the time most girls reach us,' says LPAS's Sylvia Ponsonby, 'They have been through a series of flaming hoops.' ■

No sex ads, we're British

What kind of hypocrisy is at work in a society in which contraceptive methods for men can only be advertised in magazines for woman? **Peter Freedman** reports.
October 1987

Family planning is the last of the beastly unmention-ables: the form of preventive medicine that dare not speak its name. Its lips are sealed, if not soldered together, by the restrictive codes of the advertising authorities and the selective prudery of the mass media.

Ever since Charles Bradlaugh and Annie Besant were found guilt of the corruption of public morals after publishing a birth control pamphlet in 1877, publicising family planning has not been easy. However, a spate of recent incidents has again highlighted the difficulties and shown how little we seem to have progressed.

The most publicised incident occurred last May when, after agonising for three months, the Independent Broadcasting Authority (IBA) finally banned a public service announcement encouraging teenagers to use contraception, because, as one paper put it, 'It believes young people could be influenced into thinking pre-marital sex is normal and commonplace.'

The offending item was produced by the Family Planning Association (FPA), the Brook Advisory Centres and London Weekend Television. It featured two youths talking disapprovingly of a mate who had made his girlfriend pregnant, followed by actor Adam Faith advising, 'If you're not man enough to use birth control, you're not old enough to make love.' It was to be screened after 9 p.m.

The IBA banned the announcement on the grounds that, 'It might appear to condone teenage promiscuity,' and that the language 'was likely to prove offensive to a large number of viewers'. Suzie Hayman of Brook and co-author of the script pointed out, 'It's for teenage boys and whether we like it or not three-quarters of them are sexually active by the time they're nineteen. The IBA passes one TV programme after another encouraging pre-marital sex. Look at *The Professionals*. Every week Bodie and Doyle hop into bed with a different girl, with no mention of contraception.' The FPA commented that society condemned illegitimate teenage pregnancies but was not prepared to do any-thing practical to prevent them.

The ban hit the front pages and the outcry prompted the IBA to make public a letter from chairman Lord Thomson explaining that it was not against advertisements on contraception in principle, only that particular script. In fact, a new IBA-approved version of the advertisement is now likely to appear next year.

Explains IBA Head of Information, Barbara Hosking, 'The IBA code allows for advertising of "official or officially sponsored family planning services", though not of brand-name contraceptives.' (The latter are classified along with smoking cures and haemorrhoid treatments as 'unacceptable products'.) 'The effect of this policy,' says Chairman of the Birth Control Campaign, Dilys Cossey, 'is simply to allow those organisations which under normal circum-stances cannot afford it – that is, the Health Education Council and the FPA – to advertise within tight constraints.' Those with both the will and the money for a sustained campaign, such as London Rubber (who make Durex), are pre-cluded from advertising at all. The result is that the number of family planning advertisements ever seen on television is, as IBA Advertising Controller Harry Theobalds admits, 'very small', with none at all since the seventies.

The Advertising Standards Authority (ASA), which patrols the print media in the same way the IBA patrols broadcasting, in theory treats contraceptives no differently from any other product. 'But in practice,' says Suzie Hayman, who researched its judgements for her book *Advertising and Contraceptives*, 'it applies far more moralistic standards.' This was borne out when earlier this year the ASA rejected as too sensitive two vasectomy advertisements from the charity which runs the Marie Stopes clinics. And was proved even more clearly last year by the experience of the Pregnancy Advisory Service (PAS, a charity) when it tried to publicise the new morning-after contraception.

Explains PAS's advertising agency head, Terry Johnson, 'Ads were submitted to all national papers and London Transport. Most, if not all, were fairly tasteful and quite explicit about the service being offered. We felt there would be no problem gaining approval. All the media referred the decision to the Code of Advertising Practice Committee (CAP, the copy-vetting arm of the ASA). They rejected them all as "inappropriate for this service" – even the popular "If you haven't been safe you needn't be sorry". They refused to allow us anything other than "small classified advertisements".'

'Freedom from embarrassment costs dear: last year 92,000 teenagers got pregnant and more than 3,000 girls under sixteen had abortions.'

Again, an embarrassing amount of media interest provoked CAP to announce that it had never technically banned the advertisements – although the strongly worded letters it had earlier sent to PAS allow no other interpretation. (It will be interesting to see how, or indeed if, the manufacturers of the next new birth control method – the contraceptive sponge, due to be launched early next year – will manage to publicise it.)

There was no such media exposure for PAS, however, when British Telecom informed it this year that its *Yellow Pages* entry, 'If you're happy being pregnant, fine. If not, phone …', which had been published in the 1982 edition, would no longer be acceptable in 1983. PAS pointed out that (the far from liberal) London Transport had allowed the line for many years with no complaints. British Telecom replied by citing its responsibility to eliminate 'illegal or misleading advertisements'. Though it would be difficult to get more misleading than Telecom's refusal to list PAS, which is essentially an abortion charity, under 'Abortion Services'; and its insistence on listing it instead along with other abortion services, under 'Pregnancy Testing'. Except perhaps for its refusal last year of a formal FPA request for a cross-reference in the *Yellow Pages* under 'Contraception'. The word, it was suggested, could cause undue embarrassment to the directory's readers.

What price do we pay for freedom from embarrassment?

The argument against the advertising of contraceptives is essentially that a section of the public would be offended or embarrassed by it. Perhaps it might, but then who listens to the much larger section of the public offended by, say, sexist advertising? Not, it usually seems, the advertising authorities. (A fairly typical recent complaint to the ASA concerned an advertisement in a jewellery magazine which featured a pair of scantily clad breasts with the caption, 'Why wait until your usual supplier gets his hands on them?' The ASA ruled that in the context of a trade magazine the advertisement was unlikely to cause widespread offence.)

And what price freedom from embarrassment when 92,000 teenagers got pregnant and more than 3,000 girls under sixteen had abortions last year? Suzie Hayman says, 'Momentary embarrassment can be tolerated. So often an unwanted pregnancy cannot.'

How many people would be offended anyway? A National Opinion Poll in 1979 found that 72 per cent of respondents would *not* be offended by contraceptive advertising on TV – including a majority of the over-65s. 'Once an ad does get published,' says the head of London Rubber, Janice Morgan, 'you get almost no complaints.' Suzie Hayman recalls a mid-seventies Durex campaign involving 16,000 poster sites. Most of the complaints received, she says, concerned the advertisement's

'A National Opinion Poll in 1979 found that 72 per cent of respondents would not be at all offended by contraceptive advertising on TV.'

ambiguity. 'London Rubber itself received fewer than ten written complaints and many more congratulations. Significantly, the only poster to be removed in response to complaints (on the grounds that it was situated on the main route to a school) was replaced by an advertisement for Harp lager.'

Should the advertising authorities in any case be entitled to protect us from products which are medically beneficial when they expose us so fully to others which are known to be harmful and even lethal? Alcohol and tobacco are touted on a huge scale, with fewer restrictions. And the IBA code which bans contraceptive advertising does not object, for example, to advertisements for things like war games, war comics and toy battleships.

No sex ads, we're British

International comparisons on contraceptive advertising restrictions, says Janice Morgan, show that Britain is far behind the times. And we are one of very few countries to ban the TV advertising of another 'sensitive' product, tampons.

The attitude here seems to be 'No sex ads, we're British'. Or at least when it comes to contraception and suchlike. For of course almost every product that *is* allowed on our screens – from cars to cosmetics to cigars – is plugged through the more or less crude deployment of sex. 'Sex in advertising is acceptable,' says Dilys Cossey, 'only if the product has nothing to do with sex.' And only if the subject is approached openly and responsibly is it deemed likely to cause offence. As journalist Katharine Whitehorn has put it, 'Pictures of couples in bed that would be considered innocent if advertising sheets or life insurance, are likely to give offence if they recommend contraception. It's not the picture. It's the idea.'

Double barrier methods

The advertising authorities are not the only prudes. Getting an advertisement past them is often only half the battle: in 1980 the Health Education Council had the script for a teenage contraception advertisement approved by the IBA, only for the TV companies themselves to give it such a mixed reaction that the Health Education Council decided it couldn't risk making an advertisement that might never get shown. The script was then tried out on the film censors, who gave it an 'A' certificate. But then the cinema exhibitors refused to show it except as an 'X' – which would of course have excluded the bulk of the target audience. In the end, the advertisement was never made.

The BBC is best remembered in the annals of contraceptive advertising for its heroic struggles during the seventies to keep the Durex-sponsored racing car off our screens. It refused to screen the first race in which the car was competing unless the Durex name was obscured. Then later withdrew at the last minute from another Durex-tainted race due to a sudden worry about 'the generally unacceptable level of advertising on cars'. Both London Transport and British Rail have in their time gone to equal lengths to refuse family planning advertisements, though the former has shown some improvement recently.

Those who brought us Page Three

The newspapers, for their part behave like the man who was too shy to talk to strangers though not too shy to rob a bank. Their standards could hardly be doubler. The tits-and-bum tabloids turn whiter than white at the sight of Durex ads, which are, often 'tasteful' to the point of obscurity.

'The tabloids called us salacious,' recalls Janice Morgan of one Durex campaign. Both the *Sun* and *News of the World* turned down the 1978 Durex ads 'Coming off the Pill?' and 'At last a sheath that's thinner and safer'. The *Sun*, forever brimming with tales of lusty Swedish virgins spending nights of love in converted cricket pavilions, objected to the use of the word 'sheath'. The *Daily Mail*, meanwhile, refused Durex advertisements on the grounds that theirs was 'a family newspaper'.

The Government-backed Health Education Council has behaved little better. One of its advertisements showing two pairs of feet 'so juxtaposed as to suggest sexual intercourse' under the captions 'I hope she's on the Pill' and 'I hope he's careful' were rejected by both *Sun* and *Mirror*, who felt it would 'outrage the sensibilities' of their nipple-gorged readers.

> *'The newspapers behave like the man who was too shy to talk to strangers though not too shy to rob a bank. The tits-and-bum tabloids turn whiter than Whitehouse at the sight of Durex advertisements.'*

Write on their side

The strange bedfellows of establishment distaste and popular hypocrisy are the twin barrier methods preventing contra-ceptive information getting through to us. It is a forbidding combination, but PAS's Press Officer, Helene Grahame, remains determined:

'If the arguments are marshalled, the authorities look foolish. They don't like pressure. People must write to the advertising authorities, the papers, British Telecom or their MP, saying they need and are entitled to clear information in everyday language.' FPA Director of Information, Zandria Pauncefort adds, 'Decisions about what is acceptable or not are often based on a handful of letters. Individuals *can* have a say. People should write saying they were pleased to see a particular ad or want to see more. Just one sentence will do.'

Uncovering our piano legs

'We have to move with public opinion,' says the IBA's Harry Theobalds, 'not ahead of it. We are not the FPA.' Indeed they aren't, but is there not a point when instead of moving three steps behind public opinion, the advertising authorities at least draw level with it? And when the bashfulness of the few no longer holds sway over the ignorance of the many?

There is a certain quality of surrealist satire about a society in which cinema advertisements made for teenagers are certified permissible viewing only for adults; in which the one reversible *male* contraceptive method can only be advertised in *women's* magazines; in which every product can be sold through sex except sex itself; and in which products known to kill are touted freely while those known to be good for us are kept hushed as if they were guilty secrets. It would be funnier if it weren't true and less were at stake. As it is, the joke is on the estimated 200,000 British women who had unwanted pregnancies last year.

We know that previous generations conquered their prudery at the rudery of uncovered piano legs. Surely ours could overcome its coyness at what the Government calls 'preventive medicine at its best', given the slightest chance. ∎

Brace yourself
for the backlash

Finally women are achieving! We're really getting
somewhere at work and gaining independence
at home. But some men feel we're too close
for comfort.If we believe the hype, equality is
bad for us and freedom makes us unhappy.
Only by recognising the propaganda can
we fight it and move forward.
Melissa Benn
February 1992

For the past 10 years, women in Britain and the United States
have been repeatedly bombarded with the same message: Freedom and independence will deprive you of love, marriage, children and that eternally
elusive state – happiness. No amount of achievement or progress will stop the
ticking of that biological clock. Equality is bad for you.

This, in a word, is the backlash. It's been lurking in the background for a long
time, but most of us haven't noticed it. Or we couldn't put a name to it. It was
just a niggling feeling that something was wrong – not with the world, but with
independent women.

Now it's exploding. Men's hackles are up and women are feeling powerless
and frustrated. It's still a man's world, but with one big difference. We're
confident and bright enough to realise how men are keeping us away from
power. It's just that it takes so much out of us to fight them that it's little
wonder we sometimes feel like giving up.

In a painstakingly researched and passionately written book, *Backlash*, Pulitzer Prize-winning author Susan Faludi has chronicled the ways in which American women were posted with a 'bulletin of despair' during the eighties. Much of it, Faludi argues, was a media-led male reaction to the (limited) successes of feminism in the seventies. Its aim? To prevent women from getting any further.

American women are notoriously more upfront than their British counterparts, and their brand of feminism was much brasher from the start. But we too – in our typically understated British way – have also had our successes, which have been greeted by male suspicion. We too have been subject to a rash of reports and tabloid journalism that suggest equality in all its forms is bad for you. We too have been told, 'Freedom will make you very unhappy.'

> '*Studies show self-esteem is most frequently tied to activity and/or employment and that it is married women who report higher levels of "neurotic symptoms" than their single sisters.*'

The most dominant message of the backlash has been that a single working life will only bring you misery. Throughout the eighties, the career woman, like the feminist, became subject to an onslaught of subtle, disparaging images. She had failed if she was not successful. She had failed as a woman if she was. Married women were pitted against single women, the child-free against the woman with children. No identity could ever fit properly: it always meant losing out.

Consider the crop of Hollywood films in the eighties, all supposedly reflecting the new brand of 'feminist' culture – *Broadcast News, Crossing Delancey, Baby Boom*. Yes, the heroine often had savvy and independence. Yes, she was often ensconced in corporate America. But she was also frequently neurotic, unhappy and 'selfish'. She was always concerned with getting her man and she was, in many cases, happiest of all when she had a child. On celluloid, if not in real life, babies equal nirvana.

Such imagery reached its zenith with the box office smash hit *Fatal Attraction*. Here, the single working woman was not simply desperate but positively dangerous – a potential murderer. She boiled rabbits and dropped acid on 'nice' Michael Douglas's car. Ignoring the fact that its 'happy ending' entailed the shooting of a pregnant woman, *Fatal Attraction* represented the ultimate victory of the non-working mother over the single working woman.

Even television programmes that supposedly 'tell it like it is' conceal more veiled messages. The immensely popular *Thirtysomething* took a range of 'real' women for its characters, including Melissa and Ellen, career women in their thirties. Yet once again they are too often portrayed as the sad and silly ones, constantly in awe of the saintly, stay-at-home married Hope.

The message came not just from popular culture. A number of studies, many emanating from America but given air time over here, suggested that time was up for women over 30. According to one American study in 1986, women over 30 had only a 20 per cent chance of marriage and women over 35 a mere three per cent; a statistic that Faludi resoundingly proves to be false.

Similarly, a 1982 study carried out in France, which claimed that an 'infertility epidemic' was striking professional women who had postponed childbearing, was also found to be statistically unsound.

Women have been deluged with articles, books and 'psychological' studies that suggest single and career women are subject to 'burnout' and emotional depression. Always given air time by a one-liner culture that's desperate for a new trend, a clever angle, especially on women, the more consistent findings of weighty national studies are ignored. These show that our self-esteem is most frequently linked to activity and/or employment and that it is married women who consistently report higher levels of 'neurotic symptoms' than their single sisters.

Fatal Ambition

But still the myths persist. In December 1990, producer David Puttnam told an audience of women working in the film business that women weren't rising to the top of the industry because after a hard day's work, while he could return to a wife 'who picks up the pieces', they were 'going home to empty flats and empty lives'. And in last autumn's television series, *The Men's Room*, the leading female character, Charity Walton, was finally left because she was so involved in her career.

Ambition is still seen as being not 'ladylike'. When the marriage of television presenter Anneka Rice was recently alleged to be in trouble, the *Mail on Sunday* (20 October 1991) crowed, 'Is ambition tarnishing the golden girl image?' Working women who have gone missing or who have been murdered – from estate agent Suzy Lamplugh in 1986 to 17-year-old Lynne Rogers, killed last year – are often subtly implicated through their very enthusiasm for work and independence. Reporting on a husband's conviction for an arson attack against his wife, the *Daily Mail* (24 September 1991) quoted husband Rupert Clennel-White with approval. 'She is a career girl through and through and if she wants something she will get it. Jo is very cool and calm.'

Cool, calm, uncaring, a spurner of men. Compare this to the favourable coverage of some wives and mistresses who hang adoringly on the arms of their male providers. A vast array of glamorous blondes parade through the pages of the tabloids or magazines such as *Hello!* – most of them, it would seem, once married or about to be married to the likes of Donald Trump or Rod Stewart – reminding us that a woman who can get her man is still regarded as the real winner.

The F Word

Feminism too is now under attack, standing accused of being both ball crushing and absurdly quaint. 'The new female tyrants' shrieked *Today* (4 November 1991). 'Why men won't take feminism' proclaimed the *Sunday Telegraph* columnist Minette Marrin (20 October 1991). And self-appointed leader of the male backlash, *Punch* editor David Thomas, claimed in the *Daily Mail* (31 October 1991) that 'women as well as men are fed up with doctrines of the feminist thought police'.

Even more worrying are two recent studies pointing to the negative image that feminism has among some women. Scarlett McGuire, who interviewed 200 managerial and professional women found that feminism ranked as an 'unmentionable' word among most of them.

Researcher Cynthia Cockburn, who spent two years looking at the way in which four large organisations implemented equal opportunities, says, 'Women's libbers, I was often told, are harsh, strident, demanding, uptight, aggressive, dogmatic, vociferous, radical, zealots, crusaders and overly ambitious. They have no sense of humour. They are a minority group, shouting and screeching.'

More widely, feminism is blamed for denying the 'true' natures of both men and women. Thus the rise of the new Men's Movement here and in America, urges men to get in touch with their warrior selves – literally. 'Iron Johns', so called after Robert Bly's book about men, which received massive publicity, frequently bang drums and dance round camp fires. Whereas feminists, at least according to philosopher Janet Radcliffe Richards, 'have become divorced from reality because they deny real differences between the sexes. Women may have more of a leaning towards monogamy and men to philandering …'

Similar attitudes surfaced in the discussion of last year's most hyped book, *Having It All* by Maeve Haran, in which a high-flying career woman discovered that she really wanted to be at home with her children. Women who tried to have it all – i.e. work and motherhood – were having none of it, according to Haran.

The equality myth

Of course the most disturbing assumption underlying these arguments is the biggest myth of all – that women are now free and equal; that we *do* have it all. This myth to beat all myths fuelled the arguments for much of so-called post-feminism.

'Oh, we don't need women's pages any more. Or women's magazines. Or a Ministry for Women' (recently called a Ministry for Nagging – yes, by a *female* columnist). In its good old British way, it was even part of the dispute about the changed time of Radio Four's *Woman's Hour*. Underlying that move was the view, what does it matter what women want?

> 'The voice of the feminist backlash has taken on the aura of a witch-hunt. In the popular press, it's found on the women's pages. We take offence to that; we also take offence to what they have to say.'

Let's remind ourselves of this simple fact: *most women in this country are still underpaid and overworked*. At the end of the United Nations Decade for Women 1980–1990, we clearly remain the undervalued sex.

- Full-time female workers still earn only 77 per cent of their male counterparts.
- Part-time workers, the vast majority of them women, earn even less. They also have few legal rights.
- Between 40–50 per cent of women in the workforce are ineligible for maternity rights.
- Despite Opportunity 2000, launched last October to get more women

into top jobs, women still make up only on to two per cent of senior executives. There are no women law lords. There are two women high court judges out of 82 and just 44 female MPs out of a total of 650.

• The majority of six million carers in Britain are women. Of those, 1.4 million spend more than twenty hours a week caring for elderly relatives. But only 120,000 (less than nine per cent) qualify for Invalid Care Allowance – which is currently £31.25 per week.

• Publicly funded childcare provision is virtually nonexistent. Local authority nurseries provide places for less than two per cent of children under two. Most women must still rely on, and pay for, private child minders.

• A 1990 report from the Family Policy Studies Centre, *Family Change and Future Policy*, revealed that 80 per cent of women working full time still do all the washing and ironing.

• Worldwide, women are being hit harder by the recession than men, according to a United Nations special report which was published last year (*The World's Women 1970–1990*). The UN warns that many benefits won in employment, education and health care since 1970 could be reversed because of the economic recession.

The facts point one way, the backlash points the other. The facts point to the feminisation of poverty, the backlash to the poverty of feminism. The facts point to most women today struggling to survive. The backlash says, 'Feminism is in the driving seat. Stop right there!'

No wonder women are confused. We are told by the right-wing Social Affairs unit, 'Women lack the will to compete … they do not strive as hard as men' (*The Times*, 29 April 1991). We are then told by columnist and ex-hippie Richard Neville that in the past decade women have been working so hard that 'they've grown moustaches and turned their children into strangers … all for an image of success as outmoded as the Roman Empire' (London's *Evening Standard*, 23 August 1991).

Such mixed messages have engendered a strong sense of individual failure in women. I've spoken to many women – energetic, talented and ambitious – who think they're doing something wrong. If feminism has supposedly triumphed, why do they continue to have a sneaking sense that it's still a man's world? Why, when they have worked so hard, do they still earn less than a man of comparable talent and possess so much less of that indefinable asset – status?

Doomed to failure

The backlash can only fail. It has already failed. When David Puttnam said career women had 'empty lives' he was booed by a roomful of well-rounded, achieving women. During the Clarence Thomas trial in America, when Anita Hill was ridiculed for claiming that she had been sexually harassed, opinion polls showed that she was believed and supported by women everywhere. One of President Bush's largest re-election problems is a dissatisfied female electorate.

The changes made to womens' lives over the last two decades are too deeply ingrained to be reversed. Feminism has given us access to free contraception, safe and legal abortion and, theoretically, anyway, equality in the workplace. Women may still earn only 77 per cent of what men do but the figure was nearer 55 per cent just after World War II.

Attempts to set back women's rights have failed more often than not. Last year's absurd controversy over 'virgin births' led major sperm donor centres such as the British Pregnancy Advisory Service to discontinue their AID (artificial insemination by donor) service to single infertile women. But despite repeated assaults on the 1967 Abortion Act, most of them made by the religious right-wing faction, we still retain the right to choose.

Women now consistently celebrate each other in culture. *Thelma and Louise* may have looked a bit like an extended jeans-in-the-desert advertisement, but it spoke of women riding the crest of their own confidence. In personal terms, what woman does not rank as high the eternal aims of feminism – the right of each of us to strike our own balance of work, love and friendship; the right to be our own woman?

Ironically, the backlash may sow the seeds of its own failure. As soon as it is identified for what it really is – a series of mechanisms for undermining women – we can fight it and move forward. A backlash is, after all, a powerful reaction to a powerful phenomenon. By combating it, women will rediscover their individual and collective strength. And by identifying the myths that attempt to keep us depressed and divided, we'll discover the power to act together.

Feminism is here to stay.

WHAT MEN ARE SAYING

What is real is a slow-burning male resentment against the everyday strife wrought by feminists. Men do not care that much about the whole issue; that is not just complacency, but a symptom of a much deeper syndrome: the desire for a quiet life and a hatred of being nagged. To all the feminists girding their loins for a return to the fray, there is a simple male message: 'For God's sake, give us a break, love.'

Peter Millar, *Evening Standard*, 22 November 1991

Does feminism count for anything today? Does anybody take it seriously? Some of those who do seem to take feminism seriously are not to be taken seriously themselves … As always, throughout its 25-year history, modern feminism doesn't know exactly what to think or to make of itself. According to some outward signs, it might seem that the most influential social movement of the postwar years is expiring in the last decadent gasps of redundancy.

Neil Lyndon, *The Spectator*, 23 November 1991

Most [women] do not look on men as the enemy. They live with, work with and love men. They raise young boys. They have no interest in turning men into the enemy. Meanwhile, though, men find themselves trapped by the impossible demands imposed upon them by feminism and its offshoots.

David Thomas, *Daily Mail*, 31 October 1991

Germaine Greer used to be fond of saying that women had only gained the right to say yes at the expense of the right to say no. Nowadays they are unlikely to be asked. Thanks to feminism an entire generation of men have grown up believing it's insulting to ask a girl out. Why risk being accused of treating women as objects or having a one-track mind or only being interested in one thing? As far as most men my age are concerned, you're better off watching the football.

Toby Young, *Evening Standard*, 18 November 1991 ■

The sound of violence

It's a shocking but true fact that one in four women suffers domestic violence at some time in adult life. But why are such cases of abuse still so prolific and what is being done to stop this outrageous crime against women? **Amelia Hill** reports.
November 2001

What did you do last Friday night? Spend it with friends? Have a quiet evening in front of the TV? Chloe★, a 24-year-old policewoman, did what she usually does. She rushed home from work to lay out the clothes that Justin★, her boyfriend – who also works for the force – would wear to the club that night. Then she prepared supper so she could have it ready the moment he came home. 'Then I did what I always do in those last few minutes before he comes back,' she says. 'I combed the house trying to catch anything messy or out of place that he might be able to criticise. I think of cheerful things to say to distract him and plan little ways of relaxing him. But all the time I'm doing this, I know it's useless.'

Chloe spent three years training to be a policewoman. She has learned how to deal with dangerous, aggressive men, deals with violent and disorderly men every day, and has been called out to more homes than she cares to remember. She has seen men with clenched fists tell her that the bruised woman cowering in the corner is none of her business.

And yet, for seven years, Chloe has suffered Justin's fists, kicks, and once, the blows of his riding crop in silence. She grits her teeth and continues to live an outwardly normal life as his campaign of emotional and physical abuse makes devastating in-roads into her self-confidence and the belief in her own judgement.

It's an often-repeated mantra that domestic violence spans class, wealth, religion and race. But millions of professional women of all ages still eke out lives of terror-pitted misery because they simply can't bear to confront the fact it's actually happening to them.

One in four of all crimes dealt with by the Metropolitan police involves domestic violence, and 81 per cent of incidents relate to women being attacked by men.

> 'One woman dies of domestic violence every three days in England and Wales. Millions more are living in a minefield of emotional and physical abuse.'

While the Home Office funded its Violence Against Women initiative to the tune of £10m last year, they ploughed £220m into drug-related crime and £50m alone on CCTV cameras for car parks to reduce vehicle theft.

Let's stop to think about the reality. Look around your circle of friends and consider the fact that almost one in four women suffers domestic violence at some time in her adult life. When Sandra Horley, Director of Refuge, was writing *The Charm Syndrome*, her book on domestic abuse, she found few men willing to come forwards and admit their violence. One of those who did, however, said that of eleven of his friends, every one of them had hit a woman at some time.

But if you think you'd be able to tell if one of your close friends is one of these women, think again. Two out of three women who defined themselves as victims of domestic abuse for a survey by Surrey Social Services last year, said they had not, and would not, tell family, friends or agencies about the abuse.

How many divorcees do you know? Did you know that one in three divorces involves domestic abuse? Psychologists in the US have also found parallels between the effects of domestic violence on women and the impact of torture and imprisonment on hostages. In a recent survey by the International Journal of Health Services, domestic violence was a factor in a quarter of suicide attempts by women.

One woman dies of domestic violence every three days in England and Wales. Millions more are living in a minefield of emotional and physical abuse. This is why *Cosmopolitan* is so devoted to a subject which level-headed policemen call a cancer and academics refer to as an epidemic.

The reality is that domestic violence is not a hidden crime or something that happens on the periphery of society to 'other' people. 'Of your five closest friends, it's practically a cert,' says Professor Betsy Stanko, who has been working in the area for 25 years, 'that one of them will have suffered some form of domestic abuse.' Domestic violence happens time and time again right before our eyes, bang in the centre of our comfortable lives. The only reason we don't hear the blows being struck is because we've become so familiar with the sound that we've learned to edit it out.

The men who abuse women may be dustbinmen, accountants, bus drivers or film producers,' says Horley. 'I have counselled women who have suffered terribly at the hands of clergymen, policemen and judges. On one occasion, I was horrified to find myself counselling the wife of a lawyer who support- ed our work and was at that very time involved in proceedings on behalf of an abused wife – before going home to hit his own.

What these men have in common is that they are invariably the last people anyone would suspect of abusing their partners. What is especially notable is that in more or less the same breath as they describe their humiliation and pain, most abused women talk of the loving, caring, charming side of the men who abuse them. It surprises many people to know that an abusive man can be smooth, sophisticated and charming. Often it is only when he's alone with his partner that he becomes controlling and manipulative.

Many women don't realise there is often a systematic pattern to an abusive man's behaviour, which is designed to control. He may be obsessive and isolate her from her friends. He may blame her for the abuse. Perhaps he threatens her, humiliates her in public or constantly criticises her. You don't have to be beat- en black and blue to be abused.

It has taken a long time for domestic violence to be taken seriously by the police, politicians and the media. For decades, 'a domestic' was generally regarded as an unfortunate but inevitable part of married life.

Now, however, it's front-page news. The picture of Sheryl Gascoigne three months after her wedding to Gazza in 1996, nursing broken fingers and a black eye, ran across the national press. So did Stan Collymore's attack on Ulrika Jonsson in 1998, and the legal action taken by actress Lynda Bellingham after being abused by her ex-husband for years.

The discussion has also spread into popular fiction. *Brookside*'s Jacqui Dixon was the latest soap star to have her fictional life rocked by domestic violence, in the same month that *EastEnders*' Little Mo set Albert Square humming with the news that she had finally stood up to her violent husband Trevor.

> '*For decades, "a domestic" was generally regarded as an unfortunate but inevitable part of married life.*'

Despite the turning of the popular tide, it wasn't until last year that Scotland Yard admitted 'domestics' were, in fact, serious crimes that needed to be treated as such. Now, throughout the country, support networks are springing up. Britain's general union, the GMB, recently established the Daphne Project, persuading employers to offer victims of domestic violence support. Meanwhile, the mayor of London, Ken Livingstone, has demanded the electronic tagging of persistent abusers and wants schools to accept responsibility for educating pupils about the subject.

Local community safety units were set up in every London borough two years ago, in the wake of the Stephen Lawrence enquiry, and the Metropolitan police have introduced a stream of further solutions. These include providing police with 300 cameras to photograph evidence of abuse in the home, and exploring ways of making it easier to carry a prosecution through the courts entirely on the strength of evidence collected by the police.

'In the past, the police have been guilty of being unsympathetic to instances of domestic abuse,' says Detective Chief Superintendent John Godsave, head of the Met's racial and violent crime task force. 'That was partly because they knew it was difficult to convince victims to make statements in the first place, but almost impossible to stop them retracting the statements once the case came to court.

'Domestic abuse is a cancer in our society; it will attack everywhere,' adds Godsave. 'But we feel the full picture has never been discussed.' Innovations in ways of tackling domestic violence are not just limited to London. In Liverpool, mobile phones that can make 999 calls only have been given to victims of domestic abuse. Edinburgh and Glasgow have launched a classroom campaign to educate children and the first law court dedicated to hearing cases of domestic abuse has been established in Leeds.

But experts are still concerned that not enough is being done by the government to tackle the seriousness and volume of the problem – the long-term effect it has on children, for example, and the resources it drains from hospitals and GPs.

Professor Betsy Stanko remains frustrated by the gulf between the government's eagerness to pay lip service to the issue and its unwillingness to put its hands in its pockets.

'There's more talking going on at all levels now than ever before,' she says. 'But the problem is at epidemic proportions and there's little sign that the government truly understands the enormous impact domestic violence has on society, families and services in general.'

Sandra Horley agrees. 'All too often we talk around the problem without getting closer to finding a solution,' she says.

First, we have to remember that domestic violence is a serious crime and make sure that we enforce the law. Second, we need to educate people so everyone understands what exactly is at stake. Once we all realise that we are all affected by domestic violence and have a vested interest in finding answers, it becomes easier to do something about it. Finally, we need more services, so that women have somewhere to turn. Last week, the only available refuge space in the whole country was in Leeds. During that same week, Refuge's helpline received around 7,000 calls it couldn't answer. Too many desperate women currently have nowhere to turn.

You can help silence the violence

A message to *Cosmo* readers about the government's fights against domestic violence, from Home Office Minister John Denham:

I and my colleague Sally Morgan, Minister for Women, can promise *Cosmo* readers that the government is determined to tackle domestic violence. We are working closely with the police, social services, housing departments and the criminal justice system to turn these words into action. But you, too, have an important role to play, and I warmly congratulate *Cosmo* and Refuge for a campaign that will raise awareness among young women throughout the UK.

You can find more information about what you can do to stop domestic violence in our leaflet *Break The Chain*, available from your local police station or on our website at homeoffice.gov.uk/cpd/cpsu/domestic. ■

★ *Names have been changed.*

CHAPTER 8

MEN WE LOVED

'What an uproar when a *woman's* magazine decides to have a *male* pin-up,' wrote Joyce Hopkirk in her editor's letter in April 1972.

Before news leaked out that we were photographing Paul du Feu, Germaine Greer's husband, gossip columnists had hinted that it was Alan Bates, Richard Burton, Lord Lichfield, and Oliver Reed. It seemed too ungallant to deny it. In fact, I had asked Richard Burton. A friend told me how thin he was since giving up drinking so I cabled him at his villa in Gstaad. In a couple of hours back came the reply: 'I feel the sight of this body would incite the maidens of Wales to rape the local vicar, so sadly I must decline your kind offer. Yours, fully clothed, Richard.'

Joyce maintained that 'by photographing Paul as our first male pin-up we feel we are striking a real blow for equality.' Or as Maggie Goodman, who interviewed Paul du Feu, put it: 'We think the real reason why many girls are annoyed at being considered "sex objects" is that they weren't, until recently, permitted to return the compliment.' But there was a world of difference between *Cosmo*'s coy, larky Playboys and the airbrushed aids to masturbation of the men's mags. Not that we weren't guilty of a little airbrushing ourselves – some overly-judicious retouching at the printers resulted in Paul du Feu appearing not just naked but minus his belly-button!

An English Literature graduate and construction labourer, Paul was at a loss as to how to explain his marriage to the leading feminist of the day. 'She turned up with some friends when I was standing outside a pub in Fulham Road. I suppose someone must have introduced us. She decided to come boozing with us and we ended up at my flat. And we were married a couple of weeks later.' Three weeks after that, it was all over.

Of making the history books as the first male nude in a women's magazine, Paul remarked: 'I rather like the idea of thousands of girls looking at my body. Usually before you can take your clothes off in front of a woman you have to buy her dinner and tell her how pretty she is and hope she doesn't call the police. I can't say I take it very seriously, though with all the talk about sex objects, you could say I'm striking a blow for male servitude.'

Over the next couple of years, three more brave blokes in the public eye (and a handful of male models) agreed to bare all for *Cosmo* – hairdressing superstar of the seventies, Vidal Sassoon (great body, slightly dodgy haircut); Burt Reynolds – as furry as the bear-skin rug on which he posed, and Ian – *Lovejoy* – McShane, protecting his manhood with his dachshund Morrie. The point had been made, the joke was wearing a little thin, and the rejection (most of the men who were approached did not want to strip off, even for *Cosmo*) was beginning to damage our self-esteem. Our fling with the nude centrefold had ended. Or had it?

More than twenty years later, at the peak of the lads' mag boom, when naked – or almost naked – girls had found their way down from the top shelf, and into the glossy monthly mainstream, Mandi Norwood proclaimed the return of the

male centrefold with 'an exclusive sixteen-page sealed section'. As a marketing ploy, it was brilliant. Most of *Cosmo*'s readers in the mid-nineties had been in nappies in the era of *Cosmo*'s first centrefolds. In the new age of lad's mag culture girls who, even a decade before, would have felt posing for a men's mag would damage their chances of a career, couldn't wait to get their kit off in the hope of boosting their visibility, their ratings and their record sales. Nude was no longer rude, it was something to put on your CV. Could the same be true of men?

The idea of men as sex objects was back in fashion. Even if their appearance was more likely to incite extreme fits of the giggles than spontaneous orgasms, women were queuing up to see acts like the Chippendales and the Hollywood Dream Boys, and no birthday celebration or hen-night would be complete without a male stripper-gram arriving in the pub or restaurant where the party was taking place. Mandi Norwood put it this way:

> We're celebrating our roots and giving a toast to 1973, when *Cosmopolitan* rocked the world with its most famous celebrity centrefold – a totally and beautifully nude Burt Reynolds. *Cosmopolitan*, of course, has changed with the times (as has Burt Reynolds!), but some things have remained the same … our love of men, our fascination with what makes them tick and our delight in how they differ physically from women – just think of their fabulously toned torsos and wonderfully tight butts …

Stripping open a sealed section (the nudes were no more explicit than they had been two decades earlier) was just a bit of fun – something to share with the girls at lunchtime, or when gathered round the water-cooler. If a new generation of men were up for it, why not?

Current *Cosmo* editor Lorraine Candy had considered dropping the annual June issue centrefolds, reintroduced by Mandi – until she saw the sales figures. In 2001 she teamed up with the testicular cancer charity Everyman to auction the magazine's pictures of beefcake in the buff, and raised more than £20,000 in one evening. 'So our boy pin-ups are doing more than just raising your temperatures,' she declared, at the same time as promising that the centrefold was here to stay …

In *Cosmo*'s launch edition in 1972, Jilly Cooper – already a best-selling author and columnist – was asked to nominate the men she thought would make the greatest lovers:

> Alas, I had neither the time nor the opportunity to do a bed test on any of the candidates. And as I pondered the subject I realised how

Rock-god Lenny Kravitz.

'You can leave your hat on ...' the ex- *EastEnder* Michael Greco is dressed to impress.

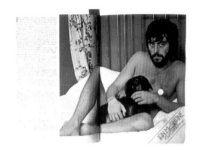

arrogant it was to assume that someone is either good or bad in bed. My conclusions must be purely subjective. What drives one girl to ecstasy may leave another stone cold. My lead balloon might be your tiger in the sack on an off day. *Lady Chatterley's Lover* may have turned her on, but you and I might have been bitterly disappointed. I've never fancied the great outdoors myself. I hate lying on pine cones, and I always get bitten to death by mosquitoes …

Her roll-call of the most likely candidates included David Niven (he of the old charm-school method of acting) because 'being a good lover means making a woman aware you fancy her rotten and, almost more important, that you think she is beautiful … After five minutes in his company, you'd feel the most desirable thing on earth – and I do like a bit of buttering-up with my bed.'

There are two types of fancying, Jilly Cooper maintained: 'Some men you hardly notice for weeks, and then suddenly the whole thing gels like mayonnaise. Others you meet and within five minutes all you can think is how much you long to be in bed with them.' Clark Gable, particularly as Rhett Butler, fell into her second category. 'Here was a man,' she wrote, 'with a million light-years of sexual experience under his belt, who'd love you and leave you, but would never put a tongue wrong while he was loving you.'

Tom Courtenay came high on her hit-list of sexy men, because she believed as a lover he'd be shy, gentle, romantic and subtle. Robert Maxwell (the publisher and MP who went on to siphon off the *Mirror*'s pension fund millions) made the grade because he seemed so nasty (and this was *before* he turned truly rotten). 'Thin little modern boys', like most pop stars, wouldn't make the grade, but big, solid men with broad shoulders and barrel chests would, and that's why Sir Geraint Evans, the opera singer, was added to her list.

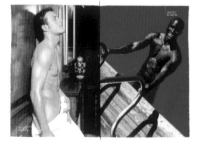

George Melly, Jilly assumed, would be good in bed because of his amazing enthusiasm for life. Roy Jenkins, because he was one of the few politicians she admired and because she would 'love to feel he was keeping a shadow cabinet waiting or letting the entire vehicle of state grind to a halt, so he could spend a few hours in my company.' The Bishop of

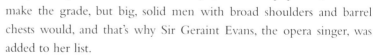

Luke Goss, of Bros fame.

OUR
SEPTEMBER
PIN-UP

Stepney, Trevor Huddleston, got an honourable mention on the basis that 'we could kick off with long sexy talks about my soul.' And finally, if group sex were called for, Jilly Cooper felt the only way to cope would be to giggle one's way through. 'So I would like Frank Muir and Dennis Nordern for my threesome, or if it were a foursome: Peter Cook and Dudley Moore and Jonathan Miller. I suppose for an orgy one would hook up with the entire Monty Python team.'

The names may have changed, but the sentiments have stayed the same. From 1972 to now, *Cosmo* has celebrated men in all their infinite variety. (And scrutinised and criticised and fault-found too, but that's another chapter). In the meantime, aaah, men …

Opposite: *Teddy Sheringham shows* Cosmo *readers his ball skills.*

CHAPTER 9

WRITE ON!

Just as feminism and lipstick were never mutually exclusive in the eyes of *Cosmopolitan*, neither were sexy and smart. Right from the start, *Cosmo*'s editors were convinced that good writing would be key to *Cosmo*'s success. The concepts of short-attention spans and dumbing-down had not yet been invented, let alone adopted by the media as a whole. It didn't occur to us that a 3,000-word article might be beyond the capabilities of the average 27-year-old. And clearly it wasn't.

If a contemporary reader of *Cosmo* were to flick through an early issue of the magazine, however, with its acres of unforgiving black and white print, and compare it to today's colourful glossies – crammed with stop-and-look-at-me photographs, the text broken-up with punchy pull-out quotes, sub-heads and side-bars, bullet-points and catchy captions, she could be forgiven for thinking early *Cosmo* looked more like hard work than reading for pleasure.

But where else were young women to go for reading that related to their lives? There were so few other modern women's magazines and the popular newspapers had hardly latched on to women's issues. The surprise, perhaps, was that far from shunning the fluffy, light-weight world of *Cosmopolitan*, serious writers were thrilled – and flattered – to write for the magazine.

In a tradition carried over from US *Cosmopolitan*'s days as a literary magazine – before Helen Gurley Brown reinvented it as the single girl's bible – *Cosmopolitan* continued to run excerpts from new novels by top authors, often printing as many as 15,000 words at a stretch. The publishers loved the idea of introducing their authors to a new, young audience, convinced it would increase book sales. The names on the cover certainly added weight to the magazine. From Erica Jong's *Fear of Flying* to Peter Benchley's *The Deep*, through the works of F Scott Fitzgerald and Tom Wolfe, Fay Weldon and Peter Carey, Doris Lessing, D M Thomas and William Boyd, *Cosmo*'s commitment to fiction also acted as a carrot in attracting other big-name writers to the magazine. 'Are you hooked on books?' we asked the readers, and annually invited some 300 of them to attend the *Cosmo* book day, at which they could meet their favourite authors, listen to discussions and readings, and find out how to go about writing – and publishing – books of their own. Authors who attended ranged from Ruth Rendell and P D James to Lisa St Aubin de Teran and the poet Craig Raine. The best-known British authors of the day were invited to review fiction, too. Over the years they included Rachel Billington, Bel Mooney, Jackie Gillott, Jill Tweedie, Penelope Mortimer and Victoria Glendinning. Derek Malcolm, the *Guardian* film critic, reviewed movies for *Cosmo* for almost 25 years. Veteran DJ Annie Nightingale was the magazine's first – and most enduring – rock critic.

In addition to using established names, Deirdre McSharry, editor from 1973-1985, determined to discover – and showcase – new, young talent. Tina Brown, who went on to edit *Vanity Fair*, *The New Yorker* and the late *Talk* magazine, wrote her first piece of journalism for *Cosmo* while still up at Oxford. 'It nearly got me sent down,' she said later, 'but launched me on a successful career of offending people in print …'

Arianna Stassinopolous, described as gorgeous, Greek and taking her PhD at the LSE, was asked to write on Henry Kissinger's dictum that 'power is the greatest aphrodisiac,' a piece which appeared in 1973 and in which she quizzed male MPs about their sex lives. For Arianna, once caricatured as 'the most upwardly mobile Greek since Icarus,' power certainly was an aphrodisiac. She went on to marry – and divorce – California Senatorial candidate Michael Huffington, as well as writing books on feminism and biographies of Maria Callas and Pablo Picasso. Also a *Cosmo* discovery was Paula Yates, who – between appearances on the cover – tried out activities as varied as weight-lifting and shopping for sex toys, and reported her findings for the magazine.

Another device for unearthing unpublished talent was The *Cosmopolitan* Young Journalists competition. Early winners included Helen Fielding, whose entry, in 1977, entitled 'Motives for Marriage' lamented the fact that all her friends had started to get hitched. Inspiration, perhaps, for her later work, *Bridget Jones' Diary*? There was Paul Keers, who eventually edited *GQ*, before starting his own publishing company, and Paul Kerton, who went to live in South Africa where he edited their edition of *Playboy*.

Cassandra Jardine became one of Britain's top newspaper feature writers on the *Daily Telegraph* and Dinah Hall became an expert writer on interior design. Laurie Graham is a successful novelist.

And then there were the *Cosmo* gurus, the writers whose names were emblazoned on the cover and whose bylines grew ever bigger along with their popularity: Irma Kurtz, Tom Crabtree, Erin Pizzey, Anna Raeburn and Marcelle d'Argy Smith, all coming to our emotional rescue with warmth, wit, wisdom, and bucket-loads of empathy. And often the kick-start we needed to make some changes in our own lives.

Certainly not in the guru category, but a distinct breed of *Cosmo* writer, were the small coterie of men – terrific journalists, ironic humour – who could explain the workings of the male psyche, and somehow make themselves look attractive in the process. It began with Christopher Ward (who went from *Daily Mirror* columnist to become head of the Redwood publishing empire) in the early seventies, trying to convince readers that men loves us for our 'bottle legs, square bums, blob noses and lopsided busts,' and went on to include, in the nineties, Michael Bywater (with his insistence that most men are bastards most of the time) and Jay Rayner (ditto), their pieces often illustrated by the brilliant cartoonist Gray Jolliffe, who did nothing whatsoever to dispel the bad impression.

During Marcelle d'Argy Smith's tenure the magazine's first – and last – political editor was appointed. Lesley Abdela, original founder of The 300 Group, was dispatched to Bosnia to report from the front on the effect of war on women's lives.

Maggie O'Kane, the *Guardian*'s war correspondent, covered the ritual raping of women in Bosnia and *Cosmo* readers were encouraged to write to Parliament and demand that rape be declared as a war-crime. Meanwhile young staff writer Kath Viner (now the editor of the *Guardian*'s much lauded Saturday magazine) was asked to display courage of a different kind, when asked by Marcelle to bare all at a nudist colony, celebrating its 50th anniversary in the UK.

In the mid-nineties, when Mandi Norwood took over as editor from Marcelle d'Argy Smith, there was an abrupt shift of emphasis. Rather than allow the writer's voice to shine through in provocative and action-inspiring essays, the magazine was re-focused to concentrate on pithier, punchier pieces in which the writer's personality took a back seat. Although the core of self-help remained, and a new generation of young writers like Wendy Bristow, Anna Maxted and Karen Krizanovich, talked openly about their own experiences, they would be remembered for their stories, but not their names. For the most part the style shifted from reflection to reportage, mirroring the fast-paced, news-oriented style of newspapers. Rather than a leisurely meal, *Cosmopolitan* became fast food. The assumption was that reading, like eating, was done on the run. The modern *Cosmo* girl would appear to be easily distracted – by ever more female-oriented newspapers and style supplements; by the plethora of TV channels, videos and DVDs on offer, by easy-read, chick-lit novels, by the internet, and of course by the 'one picture is worth a thousand words' philosophy of magazines like *Hello!* and *OK*. Sound bites came thick and fast in the form of sex tips, and stories like 'I survived a serial killer' and 'Abducted by Aliens' replaced the fiction.

Current editor Lorraine Candy has vowed to bring back to *Cosmo* some of the kudos that rubbed off from its roster of great writers. *Cosmo*'s gurus of the future, the wise women – and men – of the 21st century, the wordsmiths who can make you laugh out loud, are about to be born. Watch this space …

Girls, you and your body are driving me mad

Christopher Ward
April 1972

I wasn't in the least surprised to hear a psychiatrist speak recently of 'the profound mental anguish' suffered by girls with lop-sided busts. Even when they have textbook anatomies most women spend their entire life in a state of mental anguish about their bodies, so I can quite see how a bosom that doesn't balance up could topple its owner over the edge, so to speak.

Is there a woman in the world who actually *likes* her body? I've yet to meet a Twiggy who didn't want to look like Raquel Welch, or a Raquel who didn't wish she were a Twiggy. If a woman has a big round voluptuous bosom with enough cleavage to support a bunch of flowers, she dreams of having breasts the size of gnat bites; if a small, self-supporting bosom, she longs to be preceded everywhere she goes by a great land mass of heavy, wobbling womanhood.

Her bottom is always too fat, too low-slung or too flat. Her hips too high or too low, her legs not long enough, her mouth too big or too small, her face plain unattractive and, as for her feet … 'Have you seen my feet?' she cries. 'Don't look at them! You'll never be able to love someone with feet like mine.'

Now there would be nothing wrong with these aspirations for greater (or smaller) things, were there some grounds for discontent. But no one is complaining! And the infuriating thing is, the lovelier the lady, the more damn–

ing her self-vilification. I seem to have spent two-thirds of my love life sitting on beds trying to reassure beautiful girls that they're not nearly as ugly as they think. 'There, there now,' I say patting their hands comfortingly. 'You're not ugly. As a matter of fact …' Still, it can be very off-putting. I mean, how would you like it if some guy you've never been to bed with before suddenly says, just as he's ripping off his tie: 'You'll have to excuse my body, I'm afraid.' *Bon voyage* – too bad about the boat.

Maybe I just pick anti-narcissists, but I once had a girlfriend who actually burst into tears every time she caught sight of her naked body in the mirror. The first few times, I used to think it was me. 'What have I done now?' I'd say. 'What did I say? Was it the way I looked? Tell me! Whatever it is, I didn't mean it.'

'It's not you,' she would sob. 'It's me. Look at my body. It's so unattractive, how could you possibly fancy me?'

As it happened, she had a very pretty body, but she'd seen a few girly magazines and she had come to the conclusion that Hugh Hefner would not be writing to her inviting her to become the April Playmate. Well, he wouldn't be, but as I told her, it's not the end of the world. So we compromised. She kept her clothes on. It turned out to be an excellent therapy, because she quickly got tired of having to iron all her clothes every morning. We don't see each other these days, but friends report that she now hangs up her clothes every night.

It's a popular fallacy among other women that model girls are permanently engaged in a passionate love affair with their own bodies. Model girls certainly spend a great deal of time in front of the mirror, but in my experience, they don't much like what they see – which is why they spend so much time working on what they've got. Models are incapable of seeing themselves as they are. They can only look at themselves in comparison with other model girls. 'I wish I had boobs like Candy's.' Or: 'If only I were as slim as Sally.' Or: 'I wonder how Suzy keeps her thighs so thin.' Very occasionally, they allow themselves a pat on the back, but only at someone else's expense. 'At least my arse isn't as fat as Penny's.'

All women indulge themselves in this way to a certain extent. Haven't you noticed that whenever two couples pass in the street, the girls always look each other up and down, and never the man? Girls are far more interested in girls' bodies than men are, though for totally different reasons. Raquel Welch and Twiggy met each other for the first time recently at a reception. I didn't actually see this historic encounter between the needle and the haystack of show business, but according to an eye-witness, 'they looked each other up and down with expressions of total and utter disbelief'. And envy?

I'm married to a model, and believe me, it isn't easy. Most couples start the day with a cup of tea and maybe a piece of toast while they both bury themselves behind the papers. In our home the day starts with Mrs Ward standing naked for ten or fifteen minutes in front of the full-length mirror, examining herself from every side, unleashing a torrent of self-criticism that is positively Mao-like.

'How on earth can I work with boobs like *these*? … look how much *weight* I've put on … oh, my God, if only I weren't a *model* … tell me *honestly*, do *you* think I'm fat?'

Well, it looks all right from where I'm sitting. 'You look *fantastic*,' I say. 'Why don't you come back to bed? It's the equivalent of a three-mile run.' Some mornings I feel like a policeman talking a suicide case down from a ledge.

Would you believe that we even have rows about the way she looks? This is the way it happens:

'I look awful,' she says.

'No, you don't. You look really lovely tonight.'

'It's nice of you to say so, but you're wrong. I look dreadful.'

'NO-YOU-DON'T.'

'Don't tell *me* how I look. I *know* when I look awful.'

'Look here. I've been out with a lot of girls and take it from me, you've got nothing to worry about.'

'That doesn't say much for your taste in women, that's all I say.'

'All right then. I agree. You look a bloody sight. Your hair is a mess, you ought to lose half a stone and you need some decent clothes.'

Tears. 'I knew all along I was right.'

The other day Mrs Ward turned down the offer of quite a lot of money to appear nude in an advertisement for something unlikely like a combine harvester or a tennis racquet. I was just thinking what a refreshing change it was to find someone these days to whom money isn't everything, even though I was sharing the financial burden of these high principles, when she said: 'I mean, I couldn't have done it, could I? I don't have the figure for it.'

As a full-time unpaid psychiatrist to several dozen ladies at one time or another, I've thought a lot about this problem of why you should apparently so dislike what is so pleasing to the male eye. I used to think it was a subtle way of seeking compliments. You know the game. *You* say, 'I look awful tonight,' so that *he* spends the next twenty minutes telling you how marvellous you really are.

But it's not that at all. The unhappy truth is simply that there is no pleasing you, not with your appearance, your men, nor with little else in your lives. You don't like the way you look and no amount of reassurance from us men can persuade you otherwise. We could hand you a petition signed by 10,000 men, but if you've made up your mind to have an operation for a bigger bosom, it wouldn't stop you.

Women don't actually know what they want to look like, they just don't want to look the way they do. Why else are European women dressing up and making themselves up to look Japanese – while thousands of Japanese women are saving up the housekeeping to get together enough yen to 'Westernise' their eyes? Good heavens! Why only the other day a girl of twenty was asking a gynaecologist to restore her lost virginity on the National Health. Is there no pleasing a woman?

I wish there were some way of persuading you women that, while we admittedly love you for your bodies, we also find it possible to love you for your bottle legs, your freckles and dimples, your square bums, your blob noses and your bosoms, in all 379 shapes, sizes and half-sizes.

Would you believe me if I told you that some of my best friends have lop-sided busts? ■

What it's really like to be up at Oxford

Tina Brown
September 1973

Last year I was one of the five hundred girls to arrive in Oxford as an undergraduate – an elitist guest in a time honoured world of men. Halfway through my three-year course, the seeds of nostalgia have already been sown in earnest, and now there remains only finals to add a ferocious touch of realism. Here are a few retrospective glances …

At the beginning of my first term, queuing up for my cap and gown, I meet Sally, a kindred spirit. She wears a bright yellow scarf and scarlet dress and inhales her cigarette with long, cool movements. After dinner in Hall I ask her to my room, where over cups of coffee we talk about most things, from the Pill to neo-classicism. By the time she goes to bed we have mapped out our design for living – a dedicated oscillation between scholasticism and sensuality.

The naked walls of my cell improve with Aubrey Beardsley's black and white drawings, whilst a first look at the lecture list gives a heady sense of untapped erudition yet to come. The girl next door plays a Leonard Cohen record:

You know who I am
You've stared at the sun
I am the one who loves changing
From nothing to one.

The light goes out in the library, and the church clock tolling midnight reminds me that though it's new to me, outside this room it is all old beyond memory. An 800-year legacy of emotional energy has been lent to me by Oxford and my life is to be shaped by its atmosphere. It is the start of a glorious relationship.

Get knowledge. Get riches.
But with all thy getting, get laid.

The college motto weighs heavily on me, but for the present my mind is on higher things. At a tutorial I begin reading my essay with a flurry of self confidence:

'After a sudden *volte-face* at the turn of the century …'
'Sudden *volte-face*, Miss Brown? Are not all *volte-faces* by their very nature rather sudden? Tautologous?'

Mrs Bednerowska, an English don at St Anne's, is a formidable combination of Garbo and Voltaire, crossing and re-crossing her legs with feline elegance, exploding my Jerry-built hypotheses with one rapier thrust.

'Next week you'd better get started on Dickens' role as a social critic. You've read *Bleak House*, *Hard Times*, *Little Dorrit* and *Our Mutual Friend*, of course?'
'I …'
'Splendid. In that case, just skip through *David Copperfield*, *Dombey and Son*, *The Old Curiosity Shop* and *A Christmas Carol*. How's the Anglo-Saxon Paper going, enjoying it?'
'Well …'
'Excellent. I'll see you next week then, at the same time. Goodbyeeee …'

Back in my room I scrutinise my timetable. *Something* will have to go. It can't be Mickey's party. Or the Victorian Society; I'm practically the only member. And the Yoga classes are so good for my figure. Oh well, what if I am fat … Character is destiny, and if mine's to be a fat destiny at least it will be a well-read one.

The Trinity Players invite you to take
part in a candle-light reading. Theme
– pornography.

Tinarama, mein Liebling –
Would a soupcon of supper tonight
not be a civilised plan?
Magdalen. 7.30.

Dear Miss Brown,
The Pollution Society are looking for a
pin-up girl for their publicity campaign.
Would you mind being photographed
beside the cleanest dustbin?

Enos Stavroleon and Milos Dinossis
invite you for cocktails in the Nun's
Garden, Queen's College.

Milos's hobbies are wine tasting and grouse shooting but I don't hold that against him. Maybe I should have done. His tragedy is two-fold: he is neither English nor living in the thirties. But despite these setbacks he is determined not to compromise. His silk shirts are embellished *avec des fleurs*, while the seats in his E-type tip back to accommodate the Lotus position.

One day I make the mistake of joining him in his rooms for port and a little Mozart. Within seconds I am rushed behind a screen and told that my thighs are like honey dew. Fleeing through the quad I find the gates are locked and the porter vanished, so there is nothing for it but to climb over the wall. Two weeks later, exams loom near, and Milos complains to the college authorities that his sleep is nightly disturbed by Communists bursting into his rooms, rattling tin cans and shouting Capitalist Pig. I, the Communists and the college authorities come to an agreement. Milos's days are numbered.

'I've been reading E M Forster and I've become a Liberal Humanist.'
'I've been reading Batman and I've become a Psychopath.'

It is at the polo ball that I first meet Orlando. He has silenced the bouncer at the door by wearing a torch under a sheet of red plastic and saying he's the light show. After a term of the Grid Club and *thé dansants*, he is the first who doesn't talk about 'Wagnerian Leitmotivs' and 'Witty Little Wines'. We leave the polo ball and go on to a drag party where he expounds his own particular brand of nihilism.

'I know God's creed and we are all intrinsically nobodies. It's just that I want to be a bigger nobody than anyone else.'

Unwittingly, he has put his finger on an undergraduate obsession. At Oxford, competition is the spice of life. For Orlando, it lies in achieving more notoriety than the next man. For Sally and Cyn in editing *Isis*, the Oxford magazine; Jane, another friend, stars in the Balliol pantomime; Jenny, an ardent Socialist, starts up an adventure playground, while Vanessa, waif-like and dispossessed, grows more and more anti-establishment. Somewhere in between, I dabble first with the theatre and then with journalism, gradually aware of a pressing need to commit myself to something creative.

Outside the examination hall, Orlando sits on the wall and picks off the candidates with an imaginary machine gun, but his appeal begins to lose its magic. Gay Lib tightens its stranglehold. One evening he arrives in my room wearing more mascara than me. We drive to Whiteham Woods, and there, beneath a Lawrentian moon, we kiss and part.

'The Isis Office is going to be the Mecca of Oxford.'
'Mecca Ballroom, more like …'

It's later in the year and the female consortium has its male antagonists. But the term the women storm in is a huge success. Writing for *Isis* has undeniable perks. Armed with tape recorder and notebook I interview Oxford supermen; commissioning items for a news page results in my acquiring a delicious circle of new friends.

Suddenly we are all hooked on careerism.

Walking back from the office at 2 am we are exhausted but happy. It seems I have never felt more fulfilled or more fancy free.

> 'I love packing, now there's someone to go with me …'
> '*Soit discret*. We don't want the whole of Oxford to know …'

One by one, my friends fall in love. Cyn, once the most emancipated of *femmes fatales*, meets Tony, the dynamic ex-editor of *Isis* and becomes a reformed character. Jane, always rigorously self-sufficient and secretive about her private life disappears at intervals with a mysterious army officer. Finally, Sally starts to commission an inordinate number of articles from an extrovert classics scholar who combines stringent intellectualism with a passion for velvet suits. Only Vanessa, independent and a weaver of dreams, holds out in her determination to be a law unto herself. For me, suddenly, feminism is no longer enough.

'This is it,' I decide. 'I'm going to have the most outrageous, sensational affair, Augustian in its splendour, Jacobean in its complexity. Cataclysmic in its repercussions. We can go away together, Ireland or the Orient – and write plays, books, poems, novels, to and for and about each other.'

At the height of Spring comes Cy, riding a motor bike and writing the gossip column. His outlook reflects a curious mixture of Rudyard Kipling and *Clockwork Orange*. With him I discover the secrets of an Oxford summer. Pimms parties, strawberries, and of course, the river, a cool tunnel hung with green.

One afternoon we hire a punt and halfway between Folley Bridge and the Charwell Boat House we moor it in a secluded spot with only swans to watch us. Beaujolais; the distant sounds of voices from the Dragon School, and to left and right nothing as far as the eye can see but green fields dazzling with buttercups.

The last note of nostalgia comes from Orlando – does it summarise the whole Up-At-Oxford situation?

> What a pleasure it was to come to your Eights Week Luncheon Party.
> A veritable marathon of voluptuousness and strawberry gourmandise.
> What luxury to watch the exertions of the college rowing team, myself
> not sweating it out as I've done in the past, but sipping champagne on

our steamer – the ultimate in river-way decadence! Apparently the thirties' music drowned the count-down of the most important race of the day, but I assure you it was worth it for the guests were an enchantment and the cold collation showed huge imagination – Wow! what a spread!

My present path, from Arcadia is straight and bright with sunlight, for even as I write this letter Finals are but three days past and Heavenly choirs of wet-lipped angels speed me on my way. As I stride forth into the hard world of reality I shall remember that day on the river, and watch you acting out the rest of your dreams through rose-coloured spectacles, for as my father never fails to remind me, 'You'll never have it so good again.'

Orlando. ■

Confidence: what it is and how I learnt to acquire it

Writer and broadcaster **Anna Raeburn** conducts a weekly phone-in problem programme on London's Capital Radio and a problem column for *Woman* magazine.
July 1976

A few years ago if anyone had said that I should stand on the plinth at Nelson's Column, in all my glory on my 32nd birthday, my voice reverberating around Trafalgar Square, I would have cracked up. It was a National Abortion Campaign rally; the speakers began, and I went to the side of the stage, trying to write some details, but failing because my hands kept shaking. I'd been sick. 'You're not nervous are you?' asked one of my colleagues. 'You always seem so confident.'

I'm convinced that my particular brand of confidence is born of two things. My family taught me that it was no sin to try and fail. 'If you fall flat on your nose, you can always come home,' said my lovely parents. So many people I know don't try because the fear of failure is too great. I've always been a tryer, but I haven't *always* had confidence. The second great factor in building confidence is desperation. Only when you feel you have absolutely nothing to lose can you pitch yourself into endeavour with the kind of energy you need to reach your goal. If you really believe you're such an outsider that the odds are absurd, you may just find the kind of dash you need to carry off whatever you undertake.

You can build confidence in your profession because there's something tangible to work on. Suppose you start as I did, by being possibly the slowest typist ever to graduate from Rowlands Secretarial College in Middlesborough and you learn that if you continue to be such a snail you'll starve to death, or rather, you won't get the jobs you want, or work with the best agencies (I never did) if you're temping. There's your impetus to get better. Never think that there's only one way to accomplish a task. Perhaps you'll never be the fastest typist, but you may be reliable, neat, a good speller, particularly tactful with clients. The most important thing is to concentrate on emphasising what you've got, and to *dare* to make use of the advantages you know are yours.

I was a secretary for ten years. I had one of those cheerful, accommodating natures which made the best of everything. Then I married a man who thought I was selling myself short and who started to push me. 'But I can't do anything else,' I'd say in exasperation. 'I have no qualifications.' 'How do you think other people get their jobs?' he'd ask. 'They took what they had, blew it up a bit and got a foot in the door. Then they made good.'

> '*You can build confidence in your profession because there's something tangible to work on.*'

My first break was as a secretary-cum-researcher on an educational project. I turned in some good work and expected to be trained as an executive of some kind. Instead I was asked to be somebody's secretary again. This time I said 'No' and went home to read *The Times*, where I found the ad which led me to *Forum* magazine. An American edition was being launched and the publishers, Penthouse, were seeking three women, who could talk well on a wide range of personal and sexual subjects, to promote the magazine in the States. After two months, three of us were selected and, let me tell you, when I was offered the job I was so shaken that I refused it – and then rang back with my husband breathing down my neck to say yes, please.

That trip to the States took us to press conferences, television and radio shows of every possible format and lectures on college campuses in major American cities. It was a mercifully anonymous forcing house which meant presenting myself and my views freshly and amusingly four or more times a day. *Forum* offered me a job and, besides administering their counselling service, I talked for them as an after-dinner speaker. And in case that sounds glamorous,

I'll have you know I started doing it because money was tight and the company agreed to pay me £1 per hour for each hour after six p.m. My debut was by default when my editor had to go abroad and I stepped into the breach, speaking to 97 men. Baptism by fire! I used no notes because I can't talk without my hands and I was afraid my glasses would steam up, but my confidence grew when I learned to cover up my funny legs and make people laugh about things I felt strongly about. I was still overweight but I thought positively about Isadora's heavy arms and Liz Taylor's bosom and covered the rest with long soft dresses and tailored trousers and loose tops, remembering that 'What the eye don't see, the heart don't grieve over.'

Forum sent me to the States twice more on my own. When you travel from city to city, doing five or six radio and television appearances a day, running from station to station, working to deadlines, alone but for the PR man in that town, you must do everything you can to help yourself. The eye of the camera is sharp and you have to work with it.

You learn what make-up is vital and how much; that you need cool clothes because the lights are hot; that if you're me with my first short hairdo, lightly permed, you're going to have to allow an extra thirty minutes to use heated rollers. You learn what to eat or drink to settle your stomach because you start scared – and end scared, but in a different way.

It's easy to feel dwarfed by television, primarily because it relays an image. And television people add to that feeling of awe by asking you to arrive hours early, murmuring about make-up, depending on how much you need done and how many other people are involved; hospitality means drinking time – I don't bother; scripts concern the presenters, not the guests; and camera checks take ten minutes outside maximum. Then you say a prayer running your eye over the image on the monitor, and go.

Whether or not we know it, we all have images of ourselves. Sometimes these can be modified or altered to increase our confidence. What clothes we wear, how we dress our hair, our make-up, jewellery and other accessories can greatly change our estimation of ourselves and bring out another side of our character, what we call 'a new person'. These changes may seem superficial but long ago it was discovered that a travelling beauty salon could make people in hospital with long-term depression respond and feel better. And you know yourself how you can get up, look at a grey face and transform it into something glowing you are pleased to show the world.

Beloved outsiders are either the best help in the world or the most skilled in the art of holding us back. Haven't you at least one friend who'd look fantastic with very short hair, but whose man likes it long, so she keeps it that way? I had my hair *à la* Joan Baez, parted in the middle, varying lengths but always long, for twelve years. Exodus from that began on my 30th birthday, and since then my hairdresser, Kerry, and I have colluded in getting my hair shorter and shorter. I now know that I'm going to spend the first seven days hating the new hairstyle. Then I begin to enjoy it. In a way, this is a very good example of how long confidence takes to grow and it's a moot point which comes first – is it the change itself, or the confidence?

I keep files on various subjects, and one is full of fashion clippings to remind me I liked this sleeve or those colours or, though I'll never wear it, that beautiful hat. In that file is a photograph of the hairstyle I now have, taken from *Vogue* in 1964. In those days I worked for a doctor, one of whose patients was a very famous fashion photographer. I remember showing him the picture and asking what he thought of it for me. 'Fantastic,' he breathed. But then I weighed ten stone most of the time and wore black. Make-up was a dirty word, diets were things other people did, and I was resigned to my glasses. None of those things was unalterable, but I didn't get around to doing anything about them for ten years.

> *'How do you know when you have confidence? I suppose the short answer is when you don't stop to think about it.'*

How do you know when you have confidence? I suppose the short answer is when you don't stop to think about it. As long as you're wondering, you haven't got there – but then confidence is a bit like nirvana, a state of bliss to be striven for but rarely achieved. All sorts of human complexities intrude.

Confidence can be bluff, and the most graphic examples of this are in business. Very often the strain of maintaining a position in the competitive hierarchy of a company requires the appearance of control, and this appearance stems from self-confidence. But then this is the group of people most likely to have weight problems, drinking problems, heart attacks – all external symptoms of stress. Would they strain so much if they were confident of themselves?

However, they have a great deal of worldly and social assurance. They know the etiquette of living and they assume a uniform and a code of behaviour which makes them members of a group, part of a club. That makes anybody feel more confident, for humans are social animals, and we are basically reinforced by acknowledgement from our own.

The dictionary definition of confidence refers to firm trust, reliance and faith. Trust, reliance and faith in what? If you are experienced in a certain field, you can learn to exercise judgement. If your judgements remain sound, so your confidence grows. And confidence is like a cold. It's catching. So there is self-reliance and relying on others. Your experience tells you when and where you can rely on people. But faith brings us to the paradoxes of confidence. There is matter-of-fact faith, which echoes the previous definitions. And then there is religious faith.

Joan of Arc certainly had confidence. She was an uneducated farmer's daughter, but she believed that she could save France from the English invader. She heard voices which told her so. So convinced was she of the truth of her voices that she crossed the class lines of the day – a feat every bit as formidable as fighting off the English – and took her convictions to the Dauphin of France. She ignored the machinations of the court, the politicking and plotting which surrounded him. She believed utterly that with this faith anything was possible and she didn't falter under torture or at her burning. Vita Sackville-West wrote a magnificent account of Joan's life, drawing heavily on the translation of her own words as quoted in the transcript of her trial which align, side by side, fine examples of the humility and arrogance of her confidence. St Joan sought no reward for telling the truth. Ridiculous. But she never doubted her voices and was impatient with the doubts of others. Nowadays, many of us would simply say she was obsessed. But obsession is part of a confidence big enough to take on the stake for which we play.

Anything which demands giving evidence of ourselves in public before unknown people must necessarily demand confidence. We think of actors, politicians, film and television stars, sporting personalities, church leaders great and small, the chairman of the tenants' association, teachers, the editors of magazines – all – as possessing confidence. To some greater or lesser extent they do. But what makes them interesting is not that they have confidence captured and tied down like a handy formula kept in a back pocket for necessary occasions. It is that they falter and strive and appear confident simultaneously.

A person in the public domain who never puts a foot wrong alienates the affections of that public. We need to know that even the mighty have 'off' days, make mistakes and have to try harder. We need to know our idols are human, but also that, if they falter, they have confidence enough to recover themselves and fight back. Part of our admiration of their confidence is just because they do whatever their particular ability enables them to do in public. But for the people who exist in the spotlight, confidence is a two-way traffic. They feed the crowd or group they dominate just as they draw nourishment from the same source. Their confidence is nurtured by what is for most of us the emotional equivalent of walking a tightrope across Niagara.

It's so easy to confuse confidence with approbation. But you are not made more confident because others approve of what you do. If the corner-stone of our confidence is what other people think, then it is fragile and easily shattered. As Abraham Lincoln said, 'You can't please all of the people all of the time.' If you are truly confident, you don't seek to please but to express. And if your confidence in some aspect of your life is sufficiently strong, you can carry all before you. True confidence is impregnable, but also imper-manent. It wears down and has to be built up again. Confidence is the successful evidence of self in comparison with others, but though confidence can be estimated that way, it grows out of feelings about yourself.

'You are not made more confident because others approve of what you do.'

Some time last year, I received a letter which, like a lot of my problem page mail, was anonymous. Typewritten and clearly intelligent in tone, it asked: 'As a confident person, couldn't you write about what you'd do if …' and gave me four or five situations like, 'How would you react if you saw your husband/boyfriend talking to a really fascinating girl whose appearance and conversation you knew you couldn't top?' 'What would you say if you came into a room full of people you didn't know and felt you ought to make some opening social pleasantry?' 'How would you ever get the nerve to wear the kind of dress that would really stop the show?' What fascinated me was that the ques-tions the writer asked were dealt with at length, week by week, month by month, in every women's magazine in the country. The ideas of a new face for a special occasion, the art of agreeable small talk, how to be the life and soul of the party, keeping your man – that takes in an awful lot of beauty, social and special features, the kind of material the writer had been reading for years. The point was, she couldn't apply the information. We could all variously tell her what to do, but until she would try with enough conviction to carry it off, the words of advice were interesting but useless. There is a gap between the ideas and the application of these ideas – and you're the only person who can bridge that gap.

You don't do anything in this life if you don't want to, and you've got to want to badly – what I call 'being hungry'. Side by side with the wish there's got to be some dispassionate idea of what you've got to offer, whether professionally or personally. If you haven't got that perspective on yourself, you need either the hide of a rhino or the ego of one of Andy Warhol's superstars, and if you've either of these protections, nobody need worry about you anyway. For the rest of us, wanting something gives us the courage to try, and if we really put out, again and again, that's what our witnesses call confidence. It's to do with will and eventual skill, but there are no guarantees. Confidence may help you grow emotionally strong enough to survive the experiences, but it promises you no protection. There are no short cuts. Confidence has a lot to do with raw courage. It's no good *talking* about it – you have to *do* it. ∎

When a lovely flame dies

There was a time when tobacco tasted of
romance, when you had a drink before
and a smoke afterwards.
Marcelle d'Argy Smith mourns those heady
days of sex and cigarettes.
May 1984

I have given up smoking. I don't suppose it interests you
very much. It's of little interest to me. Giving up things isn't fascinating. But I
have to tell you that, as I stubbed out my last cigarette about six months ago,
I told myself it was a sign of the times. I stared at the stub in the brown and
white ashtray, the one that has *Buca di Santanonio, Lucca* written on it, and felt
nostalgic, wistful, older.

Because I remembered when – and they were different days – cigarettes
(dare I say it?) were romantic. They were to do with the mysteries of sex and
the fumbling beginnings of sophistication.

My first love affair began on a beach in southern France. I was stretched out
in the hazy heat of the Antibes midday sun re-reading *Tender is the Night*. My
accessories were a small bikini, blue sunglasses and a packet of Gitanes, lying
provocatively half in and half out of my beach bag. There was something
urgently attractive and worldly about a person who smoked Gitanes. The rough
tobacco was an acquired taste. But then, Gitanes smokers had usually acquired
a taste for Sartre and intense conversation. I met 'the man' when I reached

for the cigarettes. He appeared and offered me a light. He looked into my eyes and smiled. I inhaled ... and we *knew*.

We dined that evening and the smoke from our cigarettes drifted lazily in the still air of the restaurant garden. A wispy sensual intermingling. I remember our tanned bodies lying on crumpled sheets with the brilliant blue and white packet of Gitanes next to us. Cigarettes were what you did afterwards. You talked, you stroked, you lingered, you smoked. It's what anyone with even a notion of *savoir faire* did. And it was terrific, I tell you. Simply terrific.

My first affair stretched over the long French summer and into rusty autumn. Him, me and the Mediterranean-blue and white packet of Gitanes. We did everything together, we discussed practically everything you could think of. Yet the subject of heart disease did not crop up once and in our most intimate moments he never mentioned lung cancer.

Of course I had to change my brand when I came home to England. The Gitanes were too fraught with memories. And, anyway, I needed something warmer-looking to counteract London's leaden skies. Dunhill seemed to suit my mood. The shiny crimson and gold packet. Expensive, traditional, cosseted-looking. I met elegant Dunhill lighters and the men who owned them. Men with Turnbull shirts, dark suits and creative hands.

It was good to sit in Wilton's or the Connaught and gaze first at the menu and then at the packet of Dunhill on the starched tablecloth. Even if you were an absolute gourmet, the crimson and gold packet was a delicious reminder that the best was yet to come. Dunhill men sent flowers, gift-wrapped presents from Bond or Jermyn Street and asked you to marry them. Being English, they may not have understood women, but they did appreciate the subtle and wonderful difference between the sexes. These sophisticated smokers did not expect to get their women on the cheap, either financially or emotionally. The smoking bonded you somehow and they recognised this. It was easy to talk and be romantic while smoke softened the atmosphere. They inhaled and thought what they were going to say, exhaled and said it. Or you did. Dunhill meant dialogue and it was delicious. During the crimson and gold period no one accused anyone of tasting like an ashtray or having hair that reeked of smoke.

Then there were the raunchy, racy Rothmans men. A different breed altogether. Younger, more relaxed, less willing to impress. But very willing to fall in love. They were as sharp and crisp as the navy and white packet. Decisive and enthusiastic. They said, 'Let's.' And you did. You raced to crowded, noisy Italian restaurants and to each other's flats and on to planes together – because naturally you had airline tickets to romantic places. And Rothmans were smoked incessantly through all the intense interaction. You spent lazy weekends in bed making love, smoking and daring to talk about the rest of your lives. Very sensual and emotional men sometimes blew smoke rings across your body. That was heady stuff. Love, sex, optimism and cigarettes were all mysteriously intertwined.

It was harder to understand people who didn't smoke. They were accepted, of course. We were liberal. But you felt they weren't embracing the good things in life with the same uninhibited fervour as the rest of us. Non-smokers went home a little earlier, drank a lot less and married people who were 'safe'. A non-smoker *never* complained about a smoker. Non-smokers were the very opposite of the macho Marlboro man. He treated his women with a certain rough charm and he was only ever available on his own terms. He handled the sexually aggressive, scarlet and white packet with New World nonchalance and he usually used matches. When he wasn't riding cowboy country in Arizona, it was rumoured he was great in bed and amazingly gentle and tender to his Chosen Woman. I never knew one well because I was romantically involved with the Rothmans men. And you get used to a certain brand of men.

> 'We dined that evening and the smoke from our cigarettes drifted lazily in the still air of the restaurant garden.'

Then it happened. The ugly rumours were officially confirmed. Cigarette smoking was Bad for your Health. Overnight it became a dirty, anti-social, lethal habit.

Well, naturally, we all tended to ignore it for a while. Denial is a way of handling grief. Cigarettes *bad* for you? Those pure white, orally gratifying little sticks that were popped into our mouths at every meaningful moment in our lives? Those vital accessories for communication and togetherness? We carried on sucking and blowing and flicking gentle ash and saying it didn't matter. But it did. Next thing you knew was that man after gorgeous man was laying down his cigarettes and saying, 'But not for me.'

Some of the more defiant amongst us persisted for years, but it became an increasingly lonely crusade.

Romantic meals began to die a death. People thought more about their health, their weight, what they were eating and very little about their dining companion. It was hard to get personal over a Perrier and as for a cigarette – heaven forbid! Of course you sometimes had the drinks before and during the meal, but the sweet promissory note of a lingering sexual aftermath had vanished. If the topic of sex cropped up and you went home and tried it, there was no sensual chatter afterwards. It seemed that without the curly lazy smoke, the essential *après sex* atmosphere between lovers was not possible. Tender words were left unsaid. Sex, in many cases, became perfunctory.

'What of soul was left, I wonder, when the kissing had to stop?'

Not much, Mr Browning. Not much.

Well, you know the rest. It was only a matter of time before people began to lose interest in sex because sex without romance is de-personalising and depressing. A few people had sex because it was rumoured to be good for you – a form of relaxation and exercise. Heaven help us. Spinach is good for you.

Look, I'm contemporary, flexible. A 1984 person. My finger, albeit a little wobbly, is on the pulse of modern life. I understand that lung cancer, heart disease and blocked arteries are bad for your health. I read the health columns. It's terrific news that there is a breakthrough for herpes. My spirits soar. It's just that I can't help noticing that sex and cigarettes seemed to go out of fashion at about the same time and I thought I should point out that there seemed to be a very definite connection.

Think what you will, I'm wistful about the bygone era of a drink before and a cigarette after. Those golden days of Rothmans and romance, Gitanes and *je t'aime*. The days when smoke got in your eyes and men lingered over you. That era is finished, gone. Manly men are pumping iron at the local health club, getting up early to jog or do press-ups.

To hell with killer diseases. The fact is I do not want packets of painful nostalgia lying around my flat. I do not want a low tar tug at my memory. Cigarettes remind me of times that no longer seem to be available to a romantic sensualist.

And I do not wish to be reminded. So I've given up smoking. ∎

'Cor, she couldn't get enough of it …'

Even if you only gave him a goodnight kiss, by the time he tells his mates he'll have had you three times. And still you wanted more!
Jay Rayner
May 1992

I lost my virginity just a week after my 13th birthday. What a way to celebrate, eh? I don't want to boast or anything but, well, I was a natural. If I had been able, at that tender age, to play the cello the way I played that girl, I'd have been considered a child prodigy. My picture would have been in all the papers. Still, some things are best kept private, aren't they?

She was certainly my big secret: an Italian model, 23, with long dark hair, blue eyes and built like Yorkshire – all undulating hills and dark crevices. She quickly yielded to me. I was banging away for, oh, an hour at least and then, writhing with ecstasy, she asked me to stop. Of course, I obliged at once – I'm a gentleman, aren't I? So you think I'm lying? I'm not, honest. I wouldn't call it lying exactly. Embroidering the truth perhaps, a dainty piece of needlework around the edges of my life.

All right, I confess. It's a full-blown piece of tapestry. Still, you can't blame me, can you? After all, us lads must have something to brag about. So what if I didn't lose my cherry for a few more years? And so what if she came from Manchester rather than Milan? And so what if it lasted all of 35 seconds? They were a damn fine 35 seconds and I won't hear anyone say otherwise.

Such deceptions come with the territory. Bragging, just like origami or squeezing blackheads, is an art form to be practised and refined. It has its own unspoken code of ethics – a framework of rules within which its practitioners can operate, secure in the knowledge that spoilsports will never accuse them of telling fibs. Because the spoilsports will almost certainly, one day, lay themselves open to the same charge.

All men play by the rules. For a start, they will never brag about sex with their long-term girlfriends or partners. They feel there's something rather distasteful about it, akin to desecrating hallowed ground. As such relationships progress, the girlfriend very often takes on the role not only of lover, but of mother and sister too. Men don't brag about having sex with their sister.

If a man starts bragging about sex with his girlfriend you can be sure he is either seriously weird, or the relationship is on the rocks. In which case he's lying through his teeth. Sex amid the dog-ends of a relationship is a perfunctory affair, full of guilt and self-loathing. Like an appendix scar, it is not something you want to show off down the pub.

Instead, men will brag about their triumphant one-night stands, those absurd little punctuation marks in the text of their love life. Seemingly guilt-free, and so fleeting that nobody will ever have a clear idea of what really went on, the bragger may improvise to his heart's content. The one thing that we all know for sure, however, is that one-night stands are usually a disaster – two panting souls ferreting about in the dark, their true passion bound up in a straitjacket of embarrassment.

But the failings in the bragger's sex life are what frame the stories. He wants his mates to think he's as potent as they come, a veritable volcano of lust. What's more, *he* wants to believe it too. The brag is a great way of reinventing one's sex life; of editing the mental movie, taking out all the clumsiness and fluffed lines and reshooting the action sequences so that they keep the audience glued to their seats. The dignity of the woman involved is of no importance here. She is barely relevant, save that she gives the bragger a good excuse to talk about himself.

Thus the language of the brag, in keeping with its job of elevating the status of the bragger, is laced with allusions to power. A friend of mine, who claimed to have had more women in a month than he had fillings in his teeth (and his teeth were bloody awful), would always say his latest 'triumph' had been 'begging for it. She was absolutely desperate, she couldn't get enough of it.'

He was therefore not only a stud, but malevolent with it: sex had been his gift and, frankly, it had been damn nice of him to bestow it upon this invariably beautiful wench. In his stories they are always beautiful, these women, the most gorgeous babes you have ever seen. 'I had her,' he would say proudly as though she'd been his possession. 'I gave her one,' he would shout, a picture of generosity. Or if he was feeling bold, 'I gave her three.' Who's counting, anyway?

The greatest source of power imagery in the bragging world has to be the sports field. The coupling of sex with football is guaranteed to keep most men happy for hours, appealing to their pride in their stamina, skill and judgment. Thus they 'score' or 'put one in the back of the net' or even just 'play the field'. I have another friend (I really ought to keep better company) who has taken the sporting metaphor yet one step further …

'If a man starts bragging about sex with his girlfriend, you can be sure he is either seriously weird, or the relationship is on the rocks.'

He's currently 'playing the field' with extraordinary enthusiasm and luck, and claims to have enough women on the go at once to form his own five-a-side football team, with a few left over for the substitutes bench. No conversation can continue until you have found out who he has rung up to play for the coming week. Sometimes he calls them his breakfast cereal variety pack – a different flavour for every day of the week and one to spare.

He recently said that the only reason I inquired of his love life was because I was jealous. He had a breakfast cereal variety pack; I was ploughing through a sack of muesli. I knew it was good for me, he said, but I still wanted a nibble at something a little naughtier. I denied it all.

Still, he had beaten me in this round of bragging: he has them in the plural, I have them in the singular. And so the game goes on. A major part of bragging's appeal lies in its entertainment value. Just as whole villages used to crowd in to the hostelry on a cold dark winter's night to hear the elders spin folk tales, so the urban lad likes his mates to spin a few yarns. They expect it.

Recently I was sent to Amsterdam to report on the seamier side of life there for a magazine. Through a series of events too complicated and obscene to explain, I finished the trip sitting in a bath with a twenty-year-old high-class, cocaine-snorting prostitute. And I didn't do *anything*. All we did was talk. Even though I had paid the full whack, and even though she was exceptionally attractive, when the bath water started to cool I got out, dried myself off, dressed and said my goodbyes. When I got back to London nobody would believe me. How, my male friends asked, could I possibly have sat there with this gorgeous woman who was ready to have sex with me and not done anything? This was a major dereliction of duty. This was nothing to brag about. I thought it might have sounded rather weak to say I felt such behaviour would have been unprofessional. Instead I just sat there feeling guilty for not having had sex with a prostitute.

Such are the contradictions of this male sport. But there are others. For one, although the woman is vital to the whole game, she is referred to very rarely in bragging matches. All that matters is that she was present, and what took place during the event. The only female element referred to in any detail is the size of her breasts, and only then using the sort of scale usually reserved for buying loose items of clothing (small, medium or large).

And while men will happily spend hours telling one another how they were able to stay on the job and how many times they were able to do it in one session, what they will never, *ever* talk about is the size of their own genitalia. That's taboo.

Whether through homophobia or repression, they fear that telling another man about the size of their tackle will be taken as a come on. Peculiarly enough, however, men will discuss the size of each others' and take great pride in pointing out a member of their close circle who, they will say, is 'hung like a donkey'. Like every great boast this, too, is wishful thinking. Donkeys are far too well endowed for any comparison to be appropriate.

In one respect, it is totally fitting there can be no greater humiliation for a man than for his grandly constructed brag to be brought crashing down upon his head by the reappearance of the very woman he's chosen to mouth off about. That's the only occasion in his fetid love life when he is ever likely to feel like an ass. ■

CHAPTER 10

30 YEARS OF INCREDIBLE CHANGE

From politics to Pot Noodles, Maggie Thatcher to
Madonna, the events, the inventions and the people
who have influenced women's lives.

1972 The first **refuge** opens its doors in London. Founded by Chiswick Women's Aid, the refuge offered sanctuary to women and children suffering from domestic violence.

1975 National Abortion Campaign is set up to fight attacks on the Abortion Act, which had given rights to women to terminate unwanted pregnancies in 1967. The campaign's slogan is, 'Our bodies, our lives, our right to decide.'

1975 Virago, the feminist publishing house is launched and we're introduced to women writers we never knew existed. Virago publishes books that have been out of print for decades.

1976 The country's first **Rape Crisis Centre** opens, offering women a one-stop-shop for advice and counselling.

1978 Reclaim The Night demonstrations begin in the North by women against judges who give lenient sentences for rape. The slogan for the marches was, 'Whatever we wear, wherever we go, yes means yes, and no means no.'

1980 National Childcare Campaign is set up to fight for improved child-care facilities for the increasing numbers of women going out to work.

1980 The 300 Group is founded and aims for 50 per cent female representation in Parliament. There were 23 women MPs that year out of 659 seats in the House of Commons. 'Blair's Babes' increased the number to 118 in 2001. But we still have a long way to go …

1981 A small group of women captured the world's attention when they set up camp at the gates of the **RAF Greenham Common** base in protest against Cruise missiles. It became a place of pilgrimage for women with concerns about the environment, peace and their children's future.

1984 The wives of coal miners became working-class heroines overnight when they set up **Women Against Pit Closures** and found themselves presenting their case on television and in Parliament.

1988 The National Abortion Campaign fights off the Alton Bill aimed at limiting a woman's right to abortion. It is the fourth attempt to curtail the provisions of the 1967 Act by individual MPs.

HEADLINE ACTS

1973 Suzi Quatro's first UK hit, 'Can The Can', with her loud voice and leather, challenges pop's 'girlie' image of the female pop singer.

1973 Delia Smith publishes her first book, *How to Cheat At Cooking*, and the original domestic goddess is born. Delia has since taken flour power out of the kitchen and into the boardroom at Norwich City football club, and in 2001, the noun 'Delia' entered the dictionary after publishers found it had passed into everyday use.

1976 Anita Roddick opens her first **Body Shop** in Brighton. We loved her 'green' philosophy and shops sprung open across the globe.

1977 Fronting her disco-punk band Blondie, **Debbie Harry** bursts onto the music scene with lipgloss to die for.

1979 Margaret Thatcher becomes Britain's first female prime minister, but just because she's a woman, doesn't mean we have to like her.

1981 The Princess snogs her prince on the palace balcony – but they don't live happily ever after. **Lady Diana Spencer marries Prince Charles** in a flurry of cream silk and naïve optimism. If only she knew then, what we know now …

1983 Geneticist, **Barbara McClintock** is awarded the Nobel Prize for her contribution to medicine.

1983 Singer **Karen Carpenter** dies of heart failure caused by eight years of chronic anorexia nervosa.

1983 Madonna Louise Veronica Ciccone launches her pop career. She moves from punk-rock urchin to hard-nosed businesswoman and earth mother, like a cat with nine lives. Long may she reign.

1984 Soviet cosmonaut, **Svetlana Savitskaya**, 35, becomes the first woman to walk in space.

1990 British *Vogue* photographs Cindy Crawford, Naomi Campbell, Tatiana Patitz, Christy Turlington and Linda Evangelista together for its January cover – and the **supermodel** is born.

1991 Burmese human rights activist and leader, Aung San Suu Kyi, wins the Nobel Peace Prize.

1992 Yes, you can-can. Ex-dancer, **Betty Boothroyd**, becomes the first woman Speaker of the House of Commons.

1992 Nursery school teacher, **Lisa Potts**, protects her primary class from a machete attack and is later awarded the George Medal by the Queen.

1992 Stella Rimington becomes the first female Director General of MI5.

1993 Revenge for manicurist, **Loretta Bobbitt**, 24, was sweet when she sliced off two-thirds of her husband's penis after an alleged sexual assault. It was sewn back on and John Wayne Bobbitt is now a rising star in the world of pornography.

1993 Hillary Clinton, is given an office in the White House to head a health commission. It is the most influential position a President's wife has held.

1994 Patricia Marden, 37, and Eve Robinson, 70, become the first female winners in the first **National Lottery draw**, winning over £800,000 each.

1994 *Brookside's* **Anna Friel** shocks the nation with TV's first lesbian kiss.

1994 Hundreds of years of male domination in the clergy ends with the ordination of the **first female Anglican priests** at Bristol Cathedral.

1995 Prostitute **Divine Brown**, is caught giving Hugh Grant oral sex in the front seat of a car parked on Sunset Boulevard, Los Angeles. She milked the spin-offs and made enough money to retire and support her children in comfort.

1996 The Spice Girls market Girl Power and tell us what they really, really want … And they get it. Posh gets Becks, Ginger gets yoga, Sporty gets credible, Baby gets a hit and Scary gets motherhood.

1997 Princess Diana is killed in a car crash in Paris. Millions of people turn out to mourn the woman who had become a royal icon. We loved her for her honesty, her vulnerability and because we knew she cared. Britain and its monarchy have never been the same since.

1997 Helen Fielding introduces **Bridget Jones** – the world's most famous singleton and precursor of chick lit. Fielding hits a nerve; Bridget's obsession with dieting, cigarettes and men (not necessarily in that order) hides a desperate desire to be loved.

1997 Mother Teresa of Calcutta, founder of the Missionaries of Charity, Nobel Peace Prize winner and 1989 Woman of the Year, dies aged 86.

1997 J K Rowling's Harry Potter series is snapped up by publisher Bloomsbury. Rowling, a hard-up single mum, wrote *Harry Potter And The Philosopher's Stone* in an Edinburgh café. She is now worth £226 million.

1998 Spend, spend, spend! Administrator, Jacqueline King, 42, from Grimsby, is the **biggest publicised female lottery winner**, pocketing £14,003,369.

1998 Sex, lies and stains make White House intern, **Monica Lewinsky**, a household name. Her brief fling with her boss, President Bill Clinton, rocked US politics and ruined her best frock.

1998 Sunderland's **Royal National Lifeboat** Institute takes on Christina James, sixteen, as the country's first female lifeboat volunteer.

1999 Ex-model, **Heather Mills**, who lost her left leg below the knee in a 1993 car accident, is awarded the People of the Year Award for courage. Undaunted by her handicap, she has raised money for charity, and captured the heart of the world's most eligible widower, Sir Paul McCartney.

2000 Caroline Hamilton steps out into the cold and leads the first team of British women to walk to both the North and South Poles.

2000 The rock scene's wild child and mother of four, **Paula Yates**, is found dead in her home from a drugs overdose. Tragedy followed life and glamour in the media fast lane; Bob Geldof's ex found life unbearable after her lover, Michael Hutchence, was found hanged in a Sydney hotel in 1997.

2000 Julia Roberts becomes Hollywood's highest paid female star and negotiates a $20 million deal for her starring role in *Erin Brokovich* – but she still can't keep a man.

2001 Anne Robinson's *Weakest Link* proves to be her most lucrative, as she becomes television's top earner with a heavy £6.5 million pay packet.

SEX FACTORS

1970 The sexual revolution is taken one step further when women huddle around mirrors in ground-breaking **'getting to know your vagina'** classes.

1972 *Cosmopolitan* **launches**, inspiring a generation of women to find their G-spot and speak freely about what turns them on.

1972 First Ann Summers sex shop opens – primarily for men, but quickly switches to target a neglected female market with crotchless knickers and whatever else takes our fancy.

1976 *The Hite Report: A Nationwide Study of Female Sexuality* is published. Shere Hite throws presumptions on female sexuality up into the air. By questioning a random sample of women on their sex lives, her findings confirm what we knew already – that penetrative sex doesn't always end in orgasm, and that size does matter.

1976 Women share their sexual fantasies for the first time in **Nancy Friday's** *My Secret Garden*. We're surprised (or are we?) when rape is revealed as a number one sexual fantasy. Priests and doctors star in the majority of our erotic imaginings.

1978 *Our Bodies Ourselves* by the Boston Women's Health Book Collective is published in the UK. It radicalises our approach to our bodies and health – and tells us more about the female body than any doctor or mother would dare to.

1991 Sh! Britain's **first sex toy shop** specifically for women opens in London. By 2002, the bestseller is the bunny vibrator – a popular bit-part player in *Sex And The City*.

1996 *The Vagina Monologues* **by Eve Ensler** makes 'down below' the place to be and by 2001 it's a West End hit.

2001 Europe's **first brothel for women**, opens in Switzerland. Run by a former mechanic, who's roped in his mates, there's a £90 charge for a half-hour erotic massage.

LEGAL LANDMARKS

1975 Parliament enacts the **Sex Discrimination Act**, which goes into effect simultaneously with the **Equal Pay Act**. Discrimination or harassment on the grounds of gender in employment, training, provision of goods and services, housing and pay is now illegal.

1976 Women and children are given legal protection against violence in the home under the **Domestic Violence Act**.

1982 The European Court of Justice rules on **UK Equal Pay legislation** in favour of women.

1990 Justice for Women is founded in Leeds by barrister Sarah Maguire, to support and campaign on behalf of women who have fought back against, or killed, violent men.

1990 Women are allowed to be **taxed separately** from their husbands.

1991 Rape in marriage is made illegal following a long campaign by women's pressure groups.

1991 Sarah Thornton convicted for the murder of her husband, stages a twenty-day hunger strike when she learns that a man has received a two-year suspended sentence for killing his alcoholic wife. After two appeals and a retrial, she is released in 1996.

1995 Emma Humphreys wins her appeal against her conviction for the murder of her lover committed in 1985. The law is changed on provocation to allow the jury to consider the whole history of male violence – not just the final provoking act.

1996 In a sex discrimination case, **2,000 dinner ladies** in Cleveland are awarded an unprecedented £1 million payout, following a claim against their employer, Cleveland County Council.

1997 Diane Blood wins her appeal to be able to be inseminated with her dead husband's frozen sperm. Baby Liam is born in 1998.

1997 Under the Protection From Harassment Act **stalkers** can be prosecuted. One in five women is stalked.

1999 Section 41 of the **Youth Justice And Criminal Evidence Act** is introduced to limit questioning the complainant about her whole sexual history.

2001 The Government decides to **ban the date-rape drug GHB** (gamma-hydroxybutyrate) after *Cosmo* readers petition the Home Office following our 'Ban GHB' campaign.

2003 Women are awarded six months' paid and six months' unpaid maternity leave in an **Employment Bill** due to come into force in 2004.

HEALTH ISSUES

1978 Louise Joy Brown, the world's first test-tube baby is born at Oldham General Hospital.

1979 Jane Fonda goes for burn! Her first workout studio opens in Beverly Hills and by 1982, the legendary Jane Fonda exercise video becomes the best-selling video ever.

1982 First British woman is diagnosed as **HIV Positive**.

1986 US drug maker, AH Robins, sets aside $615 million to settle claims brought by users of its contraceptive device called **Dalkon Shield**. The company is forced into bankruptcy to protect itself against lawsuits brought by women claiming Dalkon Shield caused infertility.

1986 The **first at-home pregnancy testing kit** is sold over the counter.

1987 Positively Women, the first organisation dedicated to women with HIV, is launched.

1988 Nationwide cervical screening is introduced for women between twenty and 64.

1993 Nationwide breast screening is introduced.

1993 At last, a chance for us to outsmart the men who refuse to use condoms – the **female condom** is first marketed.

1993 The American Psychiatric Association votes to list **Premenstrual Syndrome** as a 'depressive disorder' in the hope this will improve treatment and improve standards for research. We all breathe a sigh of relief.

1997 The first lunchtime abortion is performed by a **Marie Stopes** clinic.

1998 Government allows women to **freeze unfertilised eggs**, and a year later says eggs can be thawed for use in IVF.

1998 The EU approves the sale of the anti-impotence drug, **Viagra**, in its fifteen member states … and pensioners' libidos skyrocket.

2000 The contraceptive pill is 40 years old. It liberated our mothers and has become the most popular form of birth control. Half of all British women aged between eighteen and 24 rely on it, along with 200 million women worldwide.

2001 The Morning After Pill goes on sale over the counter. Women over sixteen can now purchase the pill for £20, without having to see a GP.

2002 The first **contraceptive patch** to be available in the UK. Worn on the stomach, shoulders or buttocks, the patch slowly releases oestrogen and proges-terone into the bloodstream.

LEARNING CURVE

1972 Five **Oxford Colleges** agree to break with years of archaic tradition and admit women undergraduates.

1998 For the first time, more girls than boys gain **university places**.

2000 The gender gap in exam results widens as girls outstrip boys in **A Level passes**. They already outperform boys in nearly every GCSE subject.

SPORTING TRIUMPHS

1972 The Football Association reluctantly lifts its ban on women in football.